# CALIFORNIA FURNITURE

# CALIFORNIA FURNITURE

## The Craft and the Artistry

*by W. Robert Finegan*

*Picture Research by
Julie Jaskol*

*"Partners in Progress"
by Robert J. Kelly*

*Produced in cooperation with
the Western Furnishings
Manufacturers Association*

*and the Association of
Western Furniture Suppliers*

*Windsor Publications, Inc.
Chatsworth, California*

Windsor Publications, Inc.—
    History Books Division
Managing Editor: Karen Story
Design Director: Alexander D'Anca
Photo Director: Susan L. Wells
Executive Editor: Pamela Schroeder

Staff for *California Furniture:*
    *The Craft and the Artistry*
Manuscript Editor: Susan M. Pahle
Photo Editor: Robin Mastrogeorge Sterling
Editor, Corporate Biographies: Melissa Wells
Production Editor, Corporate Biographies:
    Doreen Nakakihara
Proofreader: Mary Jo Scharf
Customer Service Manager: Phyllis
    Feldman-Schroeder
Editorial Assistants: Kim Kievman, Michael
    Nugwynne, Kathy B. Peyser, Susan
    Schlanger, Theresa J. Solis
Publisher's Representative, Corporate
    Biographies: Allison Alan-Lee
Layout Artist, Corporate Biographies: TK
Designer: Thomas McTighe

Library of Congress Cataloging-in-
    Publication Data
Finegan, W. Robert, 1927-
California furniture: the craft and the
    artistry/by W. Robert Finegan; "Partners
    in progress" by Robert J. Kelly.—1st ed.
p. 136 cm. 23x31
"Produced in cooperation with the Western
    Furnishings Manufacturers Association
    and the Association of Western Furniture
    Suppliers."
ISBN: 0-89781-347-2 : $29.95
1. Furniture industry and
    trade—California—History. 2.
    Furniture—California—History. I. Kelly,
    Robert J. Partners in Progress. 1990. II.
    Western Furnishings Manufacturers
    Association. III. Association of Western
    Furniture Suppliers (U.S.) IV. Title.
HD9773.U6C245 1990
338.4'76841'009764—dc20 90-30101 CIP

Windsor Publications, Inc.
Elliot Martin, Chairman of the Board
James L. Fish III, Chief Operating
    Officer
Michele Sylvestro, Vice
    President/Sales-Marketing
Mac Buhler, Vice President
    Sponsor Acquisitions

*Right: From the early days of the 1800s, when
small manufacturing businesses created finely
crafted, handmade furniture, to the high technology of today's industry, the California furniture industry has truly experienced a long and
distinguished history. Courtesy, Western
Furnishings Manufacturers Association*

*Frontispiece photo: Assemblymen and welders
were hard at work at this circa 1955 California
chair factory. Courtesy, Western Furnishings
Manufacturers Association*

# CONTENTS

# ACKNOWLEDGMENTS

One of the most pleasurable things about researching history is the opportunity it provides to meet interesting people whose own pasts are a part of the story being told. But more than that, it is their authoritative recollections and knowledge that make it possible to better understand and put in perspective what is happening now in light of what has gone before.

Perhaps nowhere are those resources more important than when writing about such a sparsely recorded subject as the craft and art of furniture design and manufacture in California,

n industry whose birth and growth has been an important part of the phenomenal development of the Golden State.

Special thanks go to Eddy S. Feldman, a former executive secretary of the California Furniture Manufacturers Association (CFMA) from 1949-1959 and a former managing director of the Los Angeles Furniture Mart. His intimate knowledge of the industry, extensive research, and personal interviews of industry leaders have helped the author immeasurably in the organizing and writing of this book.

Three other industry

executives who also contributed much valuable information directly to the author deserve deep gratitude. They are Percy Solotoy, retired president of Brown-Saltman Furniture Manufacturing Association; Jerry Bertram, retired president of Landmark Furniture Manufacturing Company and a former president of CFMA; and Leonard M. Cohen, retired senior vice president of Cal-Mode Furniture Manufacturing Company and a former second vice president of CFMA.

Thanks also to my eldest son, Bill, who led me safely through the often bewildering world of computers and word processing; to my other sons, Mark and Roy, for listening patiently to my lengthy explanations of what I was trying to do; and to my wife, Jill, whose encouragement and endless cups of coffee kept me buoyant in more ways than one.

*Parking was just 25 cents per hour when the Los Angeles Home Furnishings Mart opened in 1958. Courtesy, Western Furnishings Manufacturers Association*

California is the largest and most exciting retail furniture market in the world. It has tremendous expansion potential that it shares with the state's overall growth rate, predicted to be the fastest in the nation during the next decade.

Recent studies show that in 1989 California accounted for nearly $5 billion in sales of furniture, home furnishings, and related appliances. This sales figure is the highest among all 50 states and exceeds even the combined New York, New Jersey, and Connecticut metro markets. Los Angeles County alone accounted for over 35 percent of that figure.

In the area of manufacturing, the furniture trade is confronted by a number of challenges, primarily because of its large concentration of factories in and around smog-plagued Los Angeles, where the furniture industry faces especially irksome regulations and controls.

Regulations include the 1983 Air Quality Management Plan (AQMP), which was revised in 1988 and formally adopted in 1989 by the Southern California Air Quality Management District (SCAQMD) to achieve an overall reduction of about 93 percent in air pollutants by 1996. The plan places costly restrictions on coatings and solvents used in the production of wood and metal furniture. Although the plan does contain specific rules, it is, for the most part, a grand strategy

for regulations that still remain to be determined.

The first phase spans five years and requires only the use of existing technologies and processes. In the future tougher emission control requirements will be phased in as better pollution control technologies are developed.

Already air pollution controls

*The Queen Anne and French influences of design are apparent in this excellent reproduction of a Federal-style bonnet top, highboy chest from New England, crafted in the early 1700s. Courtesy, Western Furnishings Manufacturers Association*

and the threat of other regulations in the future have taken a toll: In the late 1980s, a number of California furniture and cabinet manufacturers opened plants in Mexico's Baja California, and several manufacturers moved their businesses to other states.

A less serious matter, but still a concern, is the absorption and consolidation of many small furniture plants by major corporations; this trend could threaten the traditional entrepreneurial operation that has hallmarked the making of furniture in California as early as 1857. Presently, 87 percent of the plants in the Los Angeles area each employ fewer than 100 workers; the total industry work force numbers 40,000 county wide. The Achilles' heel for small manufacturers is the potential inability to cope with increasingly costly controls and regulations.

The widening of national and international markets, however, means there is room for both large and small companies to operate in harmony by carving out their own specific segments. Despite the pressures of restrictive regulations and other factors, furniture manufacturing in Los Angeles and Southern California continues to be an impressively growing industry.

The availability of low and moderately skilled labor and bargain-priced older buildings, which have become obsolete to other industries, are two factors central to the industry's growth.

While furniture sales can experience declines such as when home building dips downward, setbacks usually are only short-term detours in the industry's past and present pattern of progress.

Most importantly, manufacturers, some of whose roots go back to shortly after the Gold Rush, are dealing with their industry by using the same determination and ability to survive and prosper that is an integral part of their heritage. The story of how that heritage was shaped is the mission of this book.

Today California, as well-known for the introduction of innovative products as it is for the often outrageous and bizarre life-styles of its residents, continues the strong design influence it has long exerted on the national and international home furnishings scene. Design is, perhaps, the Golden State's most distinctive contribution, often expressed through the light colors of finishes and fabrics and the imaginative freedom of furniture shapes that reflect California's year-round mild climate and the resulting blurring of outdoors and indoors.

The story of the California furniture industry begins thousands of years ago when primitive humans, who wanted to get off the ground, cut a sturdy log straight across and then curved the wood into a cupped back. Shaped from a single piece of wood, the design included a marvelously simple and functional seat and a backrest, which in one form or another, endured throughout the ages as the basic model for all chairs.

This basic chair was a lot more; it was the beginning of the need for tables, stools, cupboards, beds, and all other utilitarian and comfortmaking necessities that the advance of civilization would demand.

Down through the centuries, the design of furniture has reflected different cultures, life-styles, and availability of various materials for its production. Ancient Egypt, for example, produced beautiful, richly ornamented furniture inlaid with silver, gold, ivory, and other precious materials. Even everyday pieces such as folding chairs, beds, and storage chests featured

*A peek into these covered wagons reveals precious bedsteads, chairs, and tables, but not all of this furniture made it to California. Much of it had to be jettisoned to lighten the load, creating a demand for replacement pieces once the settlers arrived in their new home. Courtesy, California Section, California State Library*

elegant design and some embellishment. But because of the arid climate, wood was scarce as well as costly, and domestic furniture was largely restricted to the domiciles of priests and nobles.

Often countries would borrow or adapt elements of furniture design from earlier cultures or from each other, not always with pleasing results. The Romans, for example, were influenced by the Greeks when designing the handsome Greco-Roman style of furniture, which substituted marble and bronze for wood. When the Roman Empire collapsed, so apparently did good taste, resulting in the overly ornate and unimaginative Byzantine and Romanesque designs.

Fortunately, that fallow period in the history of furniture did not last and was followed by the inventive and trend-setting Gothic era and then the Italian Renaissance, which began spreading throughout Europe in the fourteenth century. This period introduced modestly proportioned, common household furniture for the first time.

Other noteworthy design eras would come and go such as baroque, rococo, Louis XVI, empire,

*This unique elk horn chair, designed by California hunter Seth Kinman, was a forerunner of the eccentric California style of furniture design. Kinman presented this chair to Abraham Lincoln in 1864, which was duly noted in the Clerk's Office of the District Court of the District of Columbia. Courtesy, California Section, California State Library*

and a host of others. Many of these designs still inspire some of today's furniture styles, but it was the grace, lightness, and simplicity of eighteenth-century English furniture by designers such as Chippendale, Adam, Hepplewhite, and Sheraton that had the most influence on early American households.

In the late seventeenth and early eighteenth centuries, the American pioneers made their own simple furniture, which was often crude and used for strictly utilitarian purposes. The furniture was fashioned out of pine, which was easily available and soft to work with. As time passed and the East Coast colonies became better established and more affluent, the settlers began to import furniture from Europe and to reproduce the styles then popular in England.

Following the American Revolution, two furniture styles— federal and American empire or neoclassic—were developed. Neither was truly unique, since the styles were directly patterned on the work of European designers. Even the designs of Duncan Phyfe, whose discriminating taste and craftsmanship established new standards of quality and beauty, were heavily derived from abroad.

The only exception to the influence of European design was Pennsylvania Dutch wooden furniture, which was simple and often massive, and featured stylized painted decorations of animals and plants.

While all of these developments in the design of furniture were going on in the East, a whole new stage of the American Dream was beginning to unfold on the West Coast. It would, in time, result in the creation of a unique California life-style with its own special, far-reaching effect on the look of furniture, furnishings, and many other products.

# CHAPTER ONE

# STEAMER DAYS AND THE MAKING OF AN INDUSTRY

## Dreams Are the Stuff of Progress. — Anonymous

As the country slowly began to open up, more and more American colonists began to look westward. And after the first immigrant wagon train arrived in California in 1826, people began to arrive on the West Coast in increasing numbers.

The settlers piled their furniture and household goods onto ox-drawn wagons and left on long and arduous journeys toward what they hoped would be new lives and better fortune. Some of those whose destinations were in the far west never made it. Frequently immigrants set up homesteads along the way because they were attracted by the land; some turned back, discouraged by the hard and often dangerous life on the trail. Many died from illnesses, while others were unable to cope with the elements, or lack of food, or were killed by Indians. Most persevered, although sometimes they were forced to lighten their loads by casting away furniture and other treasured possessions as a necessary sacrifice to reach their hard fought goal.

In terms of California's history, the American settlers were relative late-comers. They were preceded by the Indians who had been there for an unknown length of time, the Spanish military and Franciscan missionaries in 1769, and the Mexicans who made it a province of their new republic in 1824.

The immigrants, however, quickly made up for lost time. As their trading operations in California ports began to grow, so did their desire for unity with the United States. They revolted against the Mexican government in 1846, and in that same year the United States declared California an American territory. On February 2, 1848, annexation became official when Mexico ceded the province to the United States.

During those turbulent times, furniture and other basic household needs of civilization had not yet become a pressing concern among the new Californians; they simply made do with bare necessities as they struggled to establish themselves. Richard Henry Dana, Jr., illustrated their austerity in his book, *Two Years Before the Mast*, by recording his visit to a house in Monterey in 1835.

*The houses here, as elsewhere in California, are of one story, built of clay made into large bricks, about a foot and a half square and three or four inches thick, and hardened in the sun. These are cemented together by mortar of the same material, and the*

*California settlers loaded their furniture and household goods onto covered wagons for the long and arduous journey to a new life. The rough terrain and treacherous mountain passages often forced the weary travelers to toss away some of their precious furniture in an effort to lighten the load, creating a market for new household pieces once the settlers established their new homes. Courtesy, EKM-Nepenthe*

11

*This interior view of an early gold miners' cabin shows the rough-hewn homemade cots and tables that passed for furniture in the mid-1800s. Courtesy, California Section, California State Library*

*whole are of a common dirt-color. The floors are generally of earth, the windows grated and without glass; and the doors, which are seldom shut, open directly into the common room; there being no entries. Some of the more wealthy inhabitants have glass to their windows and board floors; and in Monterey nearly all the houses are plastered on the outside. The better houses, too, have red tiles upon the roofs. The common ones have two or three rooms which open into each other, and are furnished with a bed or two, a few chairs and tables, a looking glass, a crucifix of some material or other, and small daubs of paintings enclosed in glass, and representing some miracle or martyrdom. They have no chimneys or fireplaces in the houses, the climate being such as to make a fire unnecessary; and all their cooking is done in a small cook house, separated from the house.*

Dana also described the cargo of his ship, which reflected the simple living conditions of the early settlers.

*We had spirits of all kinds (sold by the cask), teas, coffee, sugars, spices, raisins, molasses, hardware, crockeryware, tin-ware, cutlery, clothing of all kinds, boots and shoes from Lynn, calicoes and cottons from Lowell, crapes, silks; also, shawls, scarfs, necklaces, jewelry, and combs for the ladies; furniture; and in fact, everything that can be imagined, from Chinese fireworks to English cart wheels . . . of which we had a dozen pairs with their iron wheels on.*

It was a diverse list, a mix of minor luxuries and basic necessities unobtainable in the still primitive province of California.

In the early years, before cabinetmakers and upholsterers arrived on the scene, pioneer Californians either made their own simple furniture or, if they could afford it, ordered it from the eastern seaboard or from Europe. Sometimes they could trade hides and other products for furniture carried

aboard clipper ships, which had rounded Cape Horn from Boston or taken aboard overland deliveries of cargo from the East Coast at the Isthmus of Panama.

The principal destination of these ships was San Francisco and a common sight on "Steamer Days" was the crowd of retailers and individual buyers waiting on the wharf to pick up the merchandise they had ordered. Others, hoping to find articles they could purchase for themselves or for resale, would wander around inspecting the off-loaded cargo that was not consigned to see what was available.

Although the discovery of gold at Sutter's Mill in 1848 brought a huge influx of immigrants, most of them were men. By the end of 1849, the population had soared to more than 100,000, but only 10 percent were women, and the last thing in the minds of the gold miners was marrying and establishing families. All they cared about was acquiring the proper mining equipment and getting rich, which many of them did, taking more than $258 million in gold out of the ground during the next five years.

In time things would settle down as the Gold Rush petered out. In its place industry, commerce, and farming began to develop, which created and attracted families to the province, giving it the kind of stability so crucial to its future. Admitted to the Union as a free state in 1850, California's economic and population growth began to pick up following the end of the Civil War, helped by the completion of the intercontinental Union Pacific

*California pioneers often had to make their own household furnishings if they could not afford to order pieces from the East or from Europe, setting up a strong demand for local craftmanship. This settler's wagon contained chickens, pots, and blankets, but precious little room for furniture. Courtesy, California Section, California State Library*

Railroad in 1869.

By 1857 San Francisco had enough residents to support furniture manufacturing and retailing trades, along with those of many other commodities. Elsewhere in the state, major cities and seaports were emerging and agricultural communities were springing up, all creating a huge demand for houses, furniture, and household goods.

By 1875 San Francisco had a population of more than 200,000 and the city directory listed 125 furniture factories and manufacturers of bedding, curtains, lamps, stoves, rugs, and carpets.

As early as 1857, furniture and other California industries became increasingly prosperous. The Mechanics' Institute of the City of San Francisco, a society founded in 1855 for the "advancement of educational and scientific purposes," decided to put on a public "industrial exhibition" to show mostly California-made merchandise.

Cosponsored by the California Horticultural Society, the exhibition was held in a large, frame pavilion built in the shape of a Maltese cross on Montgomery Street between Post and Sutter streets. On the evening before

*The proprietors of John Breuner's Furniture Ware Rooms in Sacramento stand with their merchandise and delivery wagon on a sunny day, circa 1870, as they wait to serve the needs of local customers. Courtesy, California Section, California State Library*

opening day, September 8, 1857, Henry F. Williams, corresponding secretary of the Mechanics' Institute, promised the crowd gathered in the forecourt of the exhibition hall that the event would "develop and illustrate the rich and varied resources of our state," thereby reducing the need for "excessive importations."

Williams' next statement showed remarkable foresight about the future of the furniture industry in the state: "Permit me to mention one other branch of the mechanic arts which is being rapidly developed," he said. "I allude to the manufacture of furniture, which is now being carried on in this city profitably. The statistics furnished me by several of our largest dealers go to show that they are now able to manufacture almost every article of furniture cheaper than they can import the same."

He realized that "their operations have as yet been limited for want of workmen and the requisite facilities in the way of machinery, but their efforts thus far have been attended with marked success . . . so much so, that they assure me their chief profits for a number of months past have been upon articles of their own manufacture. That being true," he added optimistically, "it is quite obvious that the days for importing furniture into California are nearly numbered."

Noting that "our coast abounds in woods well-suited for the purpose, which can be furnished to our manufacturers at the same figures, or less, than the prevailing rates in the eastern cities," Williams said that the additional labor expense did not equal "the cost of freight and charges from Boston or New York."

Williams concluded his upbeat remarks by saying, "When we reflect that our furniture has cost us several million dollars annually, the advantages in prospect from the development of this branch of industry swell to magnifi-

*Lavishly furnished interiors like this one were no longer a rarity in California by the late nineteenth century. The demand for high quality furnishings led to the development of a local statewide furniture industry. Courtesy, California Section, California State Library*

cent proportions."

Manufacturing furniture within California was a great boost for the industry. Though the time never came when California furniture was exclusively made in the state, eventually the growth and prosperity of California manufacturers and dealers would indeed "swell to magnificent proportions."

The 1857 industrial exhibition was a huge success and would become an annual event. An even larger pavilion was erected in 1882 to accommodate the merchandise for this popular trade show. When the pavilion and the Mechanics' Institute's library were destroyed by fire in the 1906 San Francisco earthquake, the furniture manufacturers and wholesalers were left without any organized way of showing their merchandise.

Some of the award-winning manufacturers at the first exhibition in 1857 are worth mentioning for their historical interest. John Sime, president of the institute, had appointed a committee of five to select the most outstanding exhibits, which included the following furniture companies: Kreig, Geneva and Nightingale for office chairs, easy chairs, and bookcases; Frank Baker & Company for upholstered items and fixtures; J.T. Pidwell for a secretary-bedstead; George O. Whitney for parlor sets and black walnut furni-

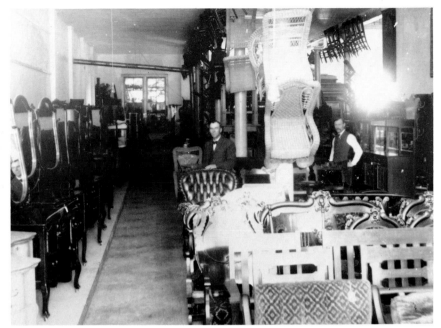

*Salesmen stand at the ready to assist customers through the maze of furnishings at this late nineteenth-century California store. Wicker chairs, vanities, and chests were just some of the goods offered for sale. Courtesy, California Section, California State Library*

ture; John Woolaver for a desk; Tottlieb Strahle for a center table with a carved pillar and feet; E.D. Waters for a chair made of manzanita and redwood; and James Taney for a "Lady's Work Box" composed of 174 individual pieces of wood, said to be taken from 30 varieties of California-grown timber.

Following the 1906 earthquake, the exhibition of furniture was haphazard and ineffective until two young men, Harry J. Moore, 33, and Thomas T. Greaves, 36, got together in 1914. Moore was the son of Hiland S. Moore, one of the founders of Sterling Furniture Company in San Francisco. Harry Moore was a buyer for the firm, traveling extensively to Grand Rapids, Michigan; Chicago, Illinois; and other eastern furniture centers. Earlier, he had started his own Harry J. Moore Furniture Company, but it failed in 1910. Greaves was also well-known in the industry as an officer of the Wisconsin Furniture Company, a retail store.

Knowledgeable about the industry's problems and having seen how they were solved in Grand Rapids, the two men became partners and rented a six-story building at 1055 Market Street. They quickly renovated it into a 50,000-square-foot manufacturers exhibition building; it was the original permanent wholesale furniture exhibition facility established in the West.

Their first Western Home Goods Market Week was held in June 1915, closed to the public but open to retailers. Twenty-eight exhibitors participated, renting spaces divided by brass rails and green curtains. They displayed furniture, rugs, coal and gas stoves, cribs, baby buggies, lamps, pictures, and ice boxes. Unfortunately, the partners' timing was off and only 16 retailers showed up to view the offerings. They had opened market week in the middle of the Panama-Pacific International Exposition, also being held in San Francisco and attracting most of the same potential buyers the new venture was seeking.

Undaunted, the young men persisted and established regular semiannual market weeks in the summer and winter. The shows became so successful that by 1917 they did not have enough space in the Market Street building, newly named "The Furniture Exchange," to handle all of the exhibitors who wanted to participate. The partners remodeled the building

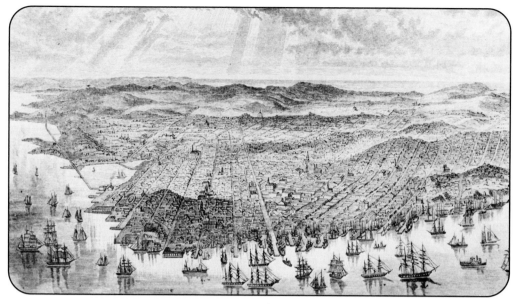

*Above: With a population of more than 200,000 the flourishing city of San Francisco was able to support a strong furniture industry by the time this 1875 view was drawn by artist J. Minton. At that time, the local directory listed about 125 different furniture manufacturers and factories, which produced a wide array of household furnishings. Courtesy, EKM-Nepenthe*

*Below: Although San Francisco held the honor of being the main furniture manufacturing center in the state in the late 1800s, the focus began to shift to Los Angeles following the devastating earthquake and subsequent fire of 1906. One of the many new furniture businesses established in Los Angeles during the early years of the twentieth century was the Philadelphia Couch Company located on Main Street. Owner Harry Siskin and an employee stand amid their inventory of tufted sofas in 1901. Courtesy, Sheldon Siskin*

and expanded the display space as much as possible, but the demand from exhibitors across the country continued to increase and the need for a larger facility became imperative.

About this same time, the focus of California furniture manufacturing, which had begun to shift from San Francisco to Los Angeles following the 1906 earthquake and fire, continued to shift after World War I. A permanent wholesale exhibition building, similar to the one in San Francisco, didn't exist in Southern California until 1934. While the Bay area remained the mecca of wholesale action for the western states, Los Angeles began tentative attempts to hold its own home furnishing shows. (Refer to Chapter 2 for more information about the development of Los Angeles shows.) Los Angeles manufacturers had even tried to organize the industry into a cohesive operation as early as 1911, when they had formed the largely ineffective Furniture Manufacturers Association of Los Angeles to deal with common industry problems.

Los Angeles area producers were on the right track though, and in 1919 their efforts resulted in the formalization of the forerunner of today's Western Furnishings Manufacturers Association (WFMA), uniting furniture

makers into a cooperative, effective organization for the first time. This 1919 organization was known as the Furniture Manufacturers Association (FMA).

Meanwhile, in San Francisco in 1920, land was acquired at 180 New Montgomery Street, near the Palace Hotel, and an eight-story building was designed and constructed in time for market week in January 1922. The response was tremendous and the tenants organized their own San Francisco Furniture Exchange Association. All 200,000 square feet of display space was rented by manufacturers from San Francisco, Southern California, and across the country. New attendance records were set.

Subsequently, the Western Furni-ture Conference was formed and located in The Furniture Exchange Building, joining the offices of several industry trade associations and trade publications. In 1931 the exchange was incorporated as the Western Furniture Exchange and Mer-chandise Mart, commonly called the Western Merchandise Mart, which later became today's San Francisco Furniture Market Center.

By 1923 Los Angeles, although still without its own exhibition building, was being hailed by *Southern California Business* magazine as "the greatest furniture manufacturing city west of Chicago." Those in the industry worked day and night and expanded plants to keep up with the demand.

*The Philadelphia Upholstering Company located at 3700 South Central Avenue in 1901 was the forerunner of the successful Angelus Furniture Manufacturing Company. Courtesy, Sheldon Siskin*

# CHAPTER TWO

# California Furniture Goes to Market

## Man Seeketh in Society Comfort, Use, and Protection. —Francis Bacon, 1605

Prior to 1911, Southern California furniture and bedding producers had no formalized organization to protect or advance their industry.

San Francisco, where furniture manufacturing had been going on since 1857, was doing a remarkable job of cooperatively promoting products to retailers nationwide through highly successful market shows. Los Angeles on the other hand, a relative latecomer to the furniture trade in 1883, was full of fiercely competitive individual producers, who ranked their business independence with the American flag, mom, and apple pie. They had not yet seen themselves as part of an industry with mutual goals and problems.

Perhaps they had grown too fast. Southern California in the late 1800s was attracting enormous numbers of settlers from the East and Midwest, lured by canny land developers and low transcontinental railroad fares. Most arrived without furniture or much of anything else except their dreams of new lives, but they soon began to set up households, creating a huge market for all kinds of necessities. As a result, more and more furniture factories sprang up in and near Los Angeles, all eager to cash in on the boom.

As the Los Angeles area replaced San Francisco as the state's major furniture production center, Los Angeles factory owners soon realized that while competitiveness obviously had its place, so did the need for unity in efforts to broaden their markets and to deal with industry problems and governmental issues. In brief, their earlier lukewarm and ineffectual attempts to organize themselves had to be replaced by a strong association with real clout and a credo of "one for all and all for one."

Subsequently, on March 24, 1919, a group of manufacturers, who were members of the Furniture Manufacturers Association of Los Angeles, met in the offices of the Hawthorne Furniture Manufacturing Shops at 1200 East Eighth Street to discuss plans to reorganize themselves into a new trade association.

According to the minutes of that historic meeting, representatives from C. B. Van Vorst Company, Manhattan Furniture Company, McClellan Manufacturing Company, Hawthorne Furniture Manufacturing Shops, Peck & Hills, Kling Manufacturing Company, Weber Show Case & Fixture Company, Angelus Furniture Manufacturing Company, Robinson Furniture

*Afternoon shoppers stroll by San Francisco's Western Merchandise Mart in 1944. An active center of the furniture and interior design trades for many years, the mart is now known as the San Francisco Furniture Market Center. Courtesy, Western Furnishings Manufacturers Association*

*Los Angeles area furniture manufacturers began to organize themselves into a cohesive unit when they established the Furniture Manufacturers Association of Los Angeles in 1911—the precursor of today's Western Furnishings Manufacturers Association. Pictured here during that fluctuating time of industry organization are workers of the Angelus Furniture Manufacturing Company in front of the East Pico factory in 1913. Courtesy, Sheldon Siskin*

Manufacturing Company, Long Beach Sash & Door Company, Inglewood Chair Company, and National Cabinet Company were in attendance.

Four important steps were taken: The Furniture Manufacturers Association of Los Angeles changed its parochial name to the all-inclusive one of Furniture Manufacturers Association, officers were elected, dues were set, and instructions issued to prepare a constitution and bylaws.

W.E. Ross, owner of Hawthorne Furniture and former chairman of the mostly defunct Los Angeles trade association, ran the meeting and was elected president of the new FMA. William I. Roberts was elected vice president, Tom McClellan secretary, and C.B. Van Vorst treasurer. C.H. Hopkins was named assistant secretary at a salary of $10 per month. Dues were established at $5 per quarter, payable in advance.

At the next meeting, held on March 31, the three officers presented drafts of the constitution and bylaws that were adopted by the membership. A creed was included in the constitution, most of which remains as pertinent today as it was then.

The overall objective spelled out in the creed was "to maintain, through an Association of Furniture Manufacturers, and allied lines, an organization for the mutual advancement and upbuilding of said industries." Beneath that umbrella was a list of specific instructions outlining how their objectives could be accomplished. The FMA required their members to promote, through personal contact with each other, an interchange of constructive thoughts and ideas; create a feeling of integrity and confidence in each other; discuss and compare labor conditions; exchange credit information and cooperate in the collection of money from common debtors; avoid duplication of each other's patterns; work and cooperate with the Retail Furniture Association of California (RFAC) on all matters for the mutual benefit of the industry; and prescribe rules and regulations for the government of members in commercial dealings.

Those tenets opened up discussions of particular concerns that surfaced at the FMA's second meeting, held on May 12. The concerns revolved

*Considered to be one of the three largest furniture trade show centers in the country today, the glamorous city of San Francisco featured the impressive Western Merchandise Mart whose elegant lobby is pictured here in 1944. Courtesy, Western Furnishings Manufacturers Association*

around such subjects as credit problems, the question of open or closed showrooms, a labor proposition (to prevent pirating of workers from each other), and general cooperation between the members. These and other ongoing problems, such as markets and high freight rates, would be dealt with endlessly by the association, just as they still are decades later.

In December 1949 the FMA was restructured and renamed as the Furniture Manufacturers Association of Southern California (FMASC). The reorganized FMASC formulated the Articles of Incorporation, which were hauntingly similar to the creed of 1919. The principal difference between the two sets of objectives was found in the industry's higher expectations and its more sophisticated perception of itself, presented as a mix of philosophical and practical goals. Objectives ranged from encouraging members "to more efficiently and profitably serve society" to "expanding the production and promoting the distribution throughout the world of home furnishings designed and manufactured in Southern California." Before the latter would happen, however, the FMA had to solve another problem.

The increased concentration of the manufacture of furniture in the Los Angeles area in the years following World War I brought with it the perennial problem of how to effectively present a product to the wholesalers and retailers. This problem was particularly troublesome since San Francisco was then, and still is, the major furniture trade show center in the state and the West. Southern California producers in search of significant numbers of buyers were forced to transport their samples 450 miles north, twice a year, to the shows in the Bay area.

Over the years, sporadic efforts would be made to establish market weeks in the Los Angeles area, using whatever locations could be leased, begged, or borrowed, but the quest eventually was abandoned in light of the attractiveness to retail buyers of San Francisco's cooler climate and glamorous image. Today the northern California city shares honors as one of the nation's three largest furniture trade show centers with Dallas, Texas, and High Point, North Carolina. Its twice-yearly winter and summer furniture shows also attract more participants than any other trade or professional convention held in San Francisco.

A former president of FMA, Herbert Iske, who had been a manufacturer's representative, recorded an example of how Southern California furniture makers depended on others for locations to show their wares.

The Retail Furniture Association of California, headquartered in San Francisco, had scheduled a meeting in a Long Beach building in 1918 and offered exhibition space around the seating area for rent by the FMA. Several factories took them up on it, including Roberti Bros. and C. B. Van Vorst, who showed mattresses; Bailey-Schmitz, Angelus Furniture Manufacturing Company, Stockwell Company, and Davis Upholstering and Furniture Company, who displayed upholstered furniture; and Manhattan Furniture Company and Hawthorne Furniture Shops, who exhibited bedroom and dining room furniture. It was one way to get exposure, but riding on the coattails of another organization's own busy event clearly was not the answer.

The following year brought another attempt, when the manufacturers themselves organized a sample showing in a building at Fifteenth and Alameda streets in downtown Los Angeles. That activity encouraged the FMA to pass a motion at its March 8, 1920, meeting to appoint a committee "to look at the ways and means of holding (another) show in Los Angeles at some future date."

Coincidentally, Robinson Furniture Manufacturing Company's new building at Fifteenth and Santa Fe streets was almost completed when the owner offered to donate space for a market week to be held from August 23 to 28. The FMA eagerly accepted, although the records reveal that they paid $1,000 for the "donated" quarters. At its July 2 meeting, the FMA enthusiastically appointed committees to handle lunches, decorations, finances, speakers, publicity, exhibits, and entertainment of the buyers. Plans were even approved to make the event semiannual.

The show was a great success, bringing in $121,000 in orders. Although it would seem that the FMA now knew how to organize shows, it was not long before the manufacturers had slipped back into their old haphazard ways of holding shows in constantly changing locations. After each weekly market, they would argue endlessly about whether there should be another one and if so, where and when it would be held.

Nevertheless, the erratic presentations continued, with one market week held in conjunction with a Los Angeles Chamber of Commerce all-industry show at the new wholesale produce terminal building on Ninth Street between Central and Alameda, while another was held in the Shrine Auditorium.

The trade shows continued in this manner for several years until 1924 when the manufacturers finally decided that they needed their own permanent industry showroom building in Los Angeles. Presumably, they were not yet ready to accept the fact that San Francisco was already firmly in place as the industry's center court for highly organized and well-promoted market weeks to attract large concentrations of buyers for their products.

Four years would pass before an FMA-leased showroom building would become a reality, and ten years would pass before the association would own its own building. In the interim, the members struggled with such controversial issues as whether the facility should be limited to Los Angeles-made furniture or be opened to samples from any part of the country, and whether they should ban operators, who instead of owning stores or inventory, used wholesale industry space as their retail outlets.

The first issue was resolved shortly before the Los Angeles Furniture Mart opened in 1935. A rumor had spread that exhibitors from places other than Southern California would not be admitted to the building. An FMA memo that said in part, "We will cordially welcome any exhibitor who properly qualifies for space," dispelled the rumor.

The second problem, which would not be put to rest for many years, was far more complicated and fraught with potential political repercussions. Several furniture manufacturers permitted freelance retailers to use their factory showrooms as stores to sell furniture to consumers. For some manufacturers this was a good source of substantial income, but to Retail Furniture Association of California members it was viewed as being in the same category as bootlegging. The RFAC coined other derogatory descriptions for these retail entrepreneurs: "ten-percenters" (from their practice of charging customers that amount over factory prices), "curbstoners," "fake dealers," and, in a desperate expression of frustration, "bloodsuckers."

Obviously not all FMA members were of similar mind about the matter, even though years earlier, in 1919, the organization had voted that "all sample rooms be closed to all dealers bringing in customers." However, a new problem arose when RFAC asked the manufacturers to refuse to sell furniture to persons they called "undesirables," using more moderate terminology than usual to describe retailers who didn't own stores.

That request had raised a thorny question of definition: What dealers were "desirable" or "legitimate"? Consequently, at the FMA's September 13, 1920, meeting, the following clarification was adopted:

*A LEGITIMATE FURNITURE DEALER is to be defined as a dealer doing business in a REGULAR STORE BUILDING with a STORE FRONT and NOT IN A RESIDENCE or UNBUSINESSFIED QUARTERS, and who does not resell or allow our furniture to get into the hands of the so-called flats or other businesses conducted in a more or less fraudulent manner.*

Seemingly that definition should have taken care of the problem, but both the FMA and the RFAC continued to gnaw on the problem. Eventually, however, they appointed a joint committee whose job it was to identify dealers who did or did not fit the designation of legitimate furniture dealer. An example of a dealer who did not qualify was one found operating out of a house at 955 South Hill Street. There is no record of what happened to him, but presumably his direct access to merchandise from manufacturers was cut off.

The subject persisted as concern rose among FMA members who saw a literal interpretation of the new legitimate dealer definition as blocking their lucrative direct sales to developers and builders. As a result, the association came up with an amendment under the heading of "Contract Business." It read that FMA and its members "consider and recognize as legitimate large Contract jobs to whom they will sell their merchandise for cash only, those whose room capacity is in excess of 150 rooms, newly equipped." Although somewhat restrictive, apparently it was acceptable to manufacturers and satisfactory to dealers.

Progress toward the goal of establishing a permanent showroom marketplace in Los Angeles took a sudden turn for the better in 1928 when several manufacturers and wholesalers leased a 12-story building at 1306 Santee Street, which today serves the apparel industry. They named it "The Wholesale Furniture Building of Los Angeles" and, with the cooperation of the owners, ran it as a "closed" (to the public) operation. A market week was held there in June 1931; the rule designating legitimate dealers was strictly observed.

In 1928 the FMA promoted A.V. MacDonald to executive secretary and he, in turn, hired Herbert Iske to handle "manufacturers relations."

Meanwhile the staff still wanted the FMA to own a showroom building. Even though the stock market would come tumbling down in 1929, marking the beginning of the Great Depression, Iske saw an opportunity to fulfill the association's long-held dream. He had discovered Citizens National Bank was about to foreclose on the 210,000-square-foot Peck & Hills warehouse at 2155 East Seventh Street. It was perfect for the FMA's needs, boasting almost 173,000 square feet of usable space, and equally important, the price was right at only $250,000.

So the search was over, but not the struggle. First there was the question of where would the money to purchase the warehouse come from? The economy was in such a state of chaos that when the FMA held a market week from January 18 to 23, 1934, it had to put a 90-day moratorium on wholesale price increases just to encourage buyers to go ahead and make purchases. In addition the Retail Furniture Association of Southern California made it clear that it wanted the FMA to stay in their present location, the leased Wholesale Furniture Building on 1206 Santee Street. Further compounding the problem, the owners of the Santee Street building were opposed to losing a lucrative source of steady income.

The only record of the financial arrangements for the Peck & Hills building is a note, apparently written in the mid- or late 1940s, and found in Iske's personal papers along with a photograph of the Los Angeles Furniture Mart. This record provides no information on how the transaction was worked out, but does describe what was done.

*Building bought from Citizens National Bank in September 1934 [actually October 2] with nothing down, nothing for 120 days after taking over the building. Then paid $3,000 a month. Borrowed $60,000 [from Citizens] to put building in shape for L.A. Furniture Mart. Paid Bank that Loan at $5,000 per month. Building clear by July 1945. Became property of the L. A. Furniture Mfg. Association who were members as of 9/20/35. No one ever put up a dime. Deal was made between me and Herb Ivey and Foster Lamby, Citizen Nat Bank.*

Considering the times and the disoriented state of the market, it was not only a terrific deal, but incredible that the FMA was able to pull it off.

Even the opposition of the retailers association suddenly and unexpectedly evaporated. Earlier in an August 28, 1934, letter, Phil Batelle, executive secretary, had informed L. C. Phenix, owner of L. C. Phenix Company and chairman of a special committee of manufacturers that the RFAC felt that

*Once
the vital center
of the Southern
California furniture in-
dustry, the first Los
Angeles Furniture Mart boasted about
150,000 square feet of space and more than
120 permanent tenants. By the time this
1950 photograph was taken, the Mart was
already overflowing its available space.
Courtesy, Western Furnishings
Manufacturers Association*

"if at all possible, the manufacturers should continue ex-
hibiting their merchandise in
the present Los Angeles
Wholesale Furniture
Building, rather than seek
some other location, possibly
not as convenient or any
more economical." The letter concluded with a note
of encouragement: "Greater
dealer support of the present, as well
as future exhibitors in this building, will be forthcoming, we feel certain."

Even as the letter was being circulated among the building's tenants by
A.E. Doty, president of the Furniture Exhibitors Association, the FMA's staff
was busily making plans in its first floor offices for the acquisition of the
Peck & Hills warehouse. Later they would move their activities into the new
building while it was being remodeled.

Whatever had been going on behind the scenes to change the RFAC's
stand is not known, but to the pleased surprise of the furniture manufacturing community, a letter dated September 12, 1934, and bearing the Santee
Street address was received from MacDonald, the FMA executive secretary.
It said, without explanation, that the retailers had not only withdrawn their
opposition to the new building, but that the FMA would be "assured of [the
retailers'] complete cooperation and patronage."

Twenty days later, on October 2, the FMA took title to the Los Angeles
Furniture Mart. So after decades of frustrations and uncertainties, the furniture manufacturers had a permanent home in which to display and sell their
merchandise.

Wasting no time, Joe Siskin of Angelus Furniture Manufacturing
Company, then president of FMA, appointed a three-man building committee to handle preparations for the Los Angeles Furniture Mart's official
opening on January 21, 1935. Its members, Ed Roberti, Roberti Bros.; K. I.
Karraher, C. B. Van Vorst Company; and C. R. Kayser, California Furniture
Shop, Ltd., were charged with establishing policy, programs, and budget.
They were authorized by the FMA's board to function unilaterally for six
months, running the mart and making decisions without first clearing their
decisions. The only monitoring of their activities, the presence of President

*Joe Siskin of the Angelus Furniture Manufacturing Company was a leading force in the preparations for the opening of the first Los Angeles Furniture Mart in 1935. Here, two shifts of wartime workers pose in front of the Angelus Furniture facility in December 1943. Courtesy, Sheldon Siskin*

Siskin at their Monday morning meetings, was by their own request.

Not all of their decisions went well. They hired a building manager, B. F. Watson, agreeing to pay him $300 a month after he had worked one month for free and one month at $50 a week. But eventually he ran afoul of the board and had to resign.

The committee, however, did make a good trade with the RFAC, offering it free office space in return for the services of a clerk to operate the admissions desk and ensure that only eligible people were permitted into the building.

All in all, a tremendous task had to be completed in a relatively brief time period. The dedicated trio not only had to oversee the myriad details of extensive remodeling, exhibition area planning, removal and replacement of equipment, and overall decoration, but had to staff the building and promote it to the industry nationwide.

The measure of the outstanding job they did is found in the response of the manufacturers: By opening day on January 21, 1935, 45 new tenants had joined the charter group of 34 FMA members for an impressive total of 79 permanent exhibitors, occupying 120,000 square feet. Those figures would

*Surveyors scout the area in downtown Los Angeles formerly known as "Washington Gardens" in September of 1956. This 4.5-acre lot, situated between Main and Hill streets, was designated as the site of the new Los Angeles Furniture Mart. Courtesy, Western Furnishings Manufacturers Association*

jump to 102 tenants using 150,000 square feet when the Los Angeles Furniture Mart held its next market week in July. Within a year, there were 121 tenants representing 300 manufacturers and the building was filled to capacity. At that time it also borrowed the successful Friday market-day pattern already established in San Francisco and Chicago.

Soon the Los Angeles Furniture Mart was the hub of the industry in Southern California. It became the source of everything connected with the trade, from official FMA activities such as promotion, freight and credit information, market shows, and special programs, to announcements of weddings, births, and deaths, and other news of the business and the people involved in it. It even became the focus of picketing for labor unions seeking visibility for their grievances.

However, new problems still developed. For example, members, who joined FMA after the mart was purchased, did not have any property ownership in the building, had no representation on the board, were assessed dues, and charged five cents per hundredweight if they used the association's Pool Car Division, a cost-saving operation that consolidated shipments of furniture from members in a shed next to the Santa Fe Railroad. Because the charter members of FMA controlled the board and paid neither dues nor fees to use the pool cars, this clearly ambiguous policy became a matter of contention, although in time it was corrected.

The mart prospered for the next few years, until it was commandeered by the U.S. Government to be used as an engine assembly plant by Lockheed Aircraft Company in World War II. The few manufacturers still producing furniture during that period found exhibition space in the Los Angeles Chamber of Commerce building at Eighteenth and Hill streets, but the pre-war heydays were gone, at least for awhile. In San Francisco, where the government also took over the industry's facilities, similar problems were being experienced.

With the end of hostilities in 1945, the furniture industry moved back into the Los Angeles building and quickly found that the mart, even though its usable space had been expanded to 172,600 square feet by an annex added by the government, still was not large enough to accommodate all of the

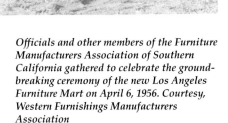

manufacturers who wanted to become tenants.

It created, in a way, a feeling of déjà vu for the FMA. Once more manufacturers faced a space problem; one they thought they had solved. There were three choices for dealing with this problem: expand on the existing lot, return to limiting tenancy to local manufacturers, or find a larger building at another location.

*Officials and other members of the Furniture Manufacturers Association of Southern California gathered to celebrate the ground-breaking ceremony of the new Los Angeles Furniture Mart on April 6, 1956. Courtesy, Western Furnishings Manufacturers Association*

Riding high on the post-war boom, many local manufacturers felt that it no longer made sense to provide exhibit space to eastern and southern competitors, but the FMA board took no action on that or either of the other two proposals, but did act in 1949 to change its name by adding Southern California to FMA thus becoming FMASC.

Unable to get into the now bulging Los Angeles Furniture Mart, a number of local representatives from East Coast manufacturers of furniture and accessories bought a building at 533 South Los Angeles Street and named it the Furniture Manufacturers Mart, which they operated until 1958 when a greatly expanded Los Angeles Furniture Mart was opened by the now newly named FMA of California. Other exhibitors, who were unable to get into the mart on a permanent basis, were helped by the FMAC during market times through temporary shows held in the Shrine Exposition Hall, a stopgap that lasted for the next five years.

To FMAC's MacDonald and John H. Graves, a former retail executive who was in charge of the association's retailer relations, there was only one practical answer to this space problem caused by the industry's tremendous success: Construct a new Los Angeles Furniture Mart building.

The two men organized the Los Angeles Furniture Mart Building Corporation in 1948 to purchase a 4.5-acre vacant lot known as "Washington Gardens" south of Washington Boulevard to Twenty-first Street and between Main and Hill streets. Located only a few blocks from a site considered by the old FMA for a permanent building in 1922, the land had been owned in the 1880s by David E. Waldron, who placed on it a theater, an octagon pavilion, a menagerie, and a shooting gallery, along with a variety of fruit trees. Later the gardens would be used for baseball, circuses, automobile shows, and evangelistic meetings, but it was now the last available property of its size in the city of Los Angeles.

*Percy Solotoy, president of Brown-Saltman Furniture Manufacturing Company in South Gate, served as the president of the Furniture Manufacturers Association during the tumultuous year of 1947-1948. Pictured here with a visitor from the Philippines at the Brown-Saltman facilities in 1963, Solotoy's unflagging support for the new Los Angeles Furniture Mart was crucial to its success. Courtesy, Western Furnishings Manufacturers Association*

MacDonald and Graves set out to raise money for the purchase and soon had $150,000 contributed by manufacturers, manufacturers' representatives, and others in the industry. Filled with confidence, they retained two architects, Earl Heitschmidt and Whiting S. Thompson, to design an innovative and mammoth two-million-square-foot structure. Unfortunately, a critical ingredient was missing, namely the approval and support of the FMA, which was not forthcoming.

Shortly after running into that roadblock, the pair ran out of money and could not meet the option payment. Because those manufacturers who already were shareholders in the Los Angeles Furniture Mart refused to lease space in the proposed building, the new corporation could not obtain financing. The FMA essentially was split down the middle, some members feeling MacDonald and Graves had the right idea, but others were vehemently opposed because the present mart was doing just fine and they were reluctant to jeopardize it.

Following an acrid debate among the share-holding FMASC members meeting in the mart's basement on September 25, 1951, it was decided that they would assume the assets and liabilities of the floundering Furniture Mart Building Corporation. They made the payment on the land option and also took over the engineering studies and architectural plans. Once again everything looked hopeful.

However, no great effort was made to get the project back on track until R.W. Potter was elected president of FMASC in 1954. Potter was a 59-year-old Englishman who had emigrated to Canada after World War I and then to the Los Angeles area in 1927, where he was vice president and general manager of Brown-Saltman Furniture Manufacturing Company in South Gate. Brown-Saltman's president was Percy Solotoy, who had been president of FMA during the stormy year of 1947-48 and he, along with Potter, MacDonald, and Graves, firmly believed in the need for a new building. Indeed, so convinced was Solotoy that he loaned Potter to the project on an almost full-time basis.

It was a good move for all concerned. Potter used his charm and persuasiveness to get Prudential Insurance Company to buy the property after the new mart was built, and then he went to the Bank of America for interim

*Construction of the 12-story Los Angeles Furniture Mart nears its final phase in the autumn of 1957. Courtesy, Western Furnishings Manufacturers Association*

financing. The deal was that FMASC would lease the building for 25 years, plus have four 10-year options, for a total of 65 years. But there were a few obstacles to overcome before construction could begin. The major one was a requirement by Prudential that 90 percent of the mart's 867,000 square feet of rentable space be leased in advance on 10-year leases—a formidable challenge—particularly since it would have to be met before the building even existed.

Potter, aided by MacDonald, Graves, and Edward King, a man highly regarded in the industry, promptly proceeded to achieve the seemingly impossible. Within a few months they had signed the necessary advance tenants, including lamp and shade manufacturers and the widely scattered floor covering businesses, some of whom had even committed to moving their headquarters to Los Angeles from San Francisco.

On April 6, 1958, ground was broken for the new 12-story mart, which when completed, would be the largest reinforced concrete structure in Los Angeles in those days. Lieutenant Governor Harold J. Powers remarked at the ceremony that the building "symbolized at once the depth of their [the furniture industry's] vision and their confidence in the future." It was a triumphal moment.

Other welcome news would follow. The old Los Angeles Furniture Mart on Santee Street, which had closed its doors on March 30, 1958, was sold by FMAC to Sweetheart Cup Corporation for $500,000.

Shortly before the new Los Angeles Furniture Mart held its first market week on July 14, 1958, MacDonald decided it was time to retire. He died on December 14, 1963, in the Baldwin Hills dam disaster. Eddy S. Feldman, then executive secretary of FMAC, was named to succeed him as managing director, a post he would occupy until 1974. Potter, who each year had been re-elected president of FMAC, became ill and died in 1960. While in the hospital he had asked Herman Kranz, vice president of the FMA board and president of Morris Furniture Manufacturing Company, to take over the leadership of the association.

Once more the mart, the center of the industry, flourished and introduced several innovative changes. One, put forward by Herbert E. Toor,

acknowledged the distant locations of some dealers in the western states. Fridays were traditionally established as market days, but the building was also opened on the last Thursday of every month to make their travel worthwhile. Another change involved beginning the mart's market weeks on Sundays instead of the traditional Mondays, an idea soon copied by others.

Cooperation between San Francisco and Los Angeles also took a big step forward in those years. Many of the manufacturers were tenants in the market buildings in both cities and an arrangement was made to stagger the showings so they would not conflict with each other. Since the market weeks no longer coincided, another benefit was that only one set of samples was needed instead of two. As one market week ended, a cavalcade of trucks and trailers would wend its way north or south to the next show.

But in the end, it was that very same coordination that spotlighted the impracticality of continuing to have permanent industry show buildings in two different locations in the state. In 1968 the original 10-year tenant leases in the Los Angeles Furniture Mart expired, and many of the southern manufacturers seized the opportunity to pull out. They kept their spaces in the Western Merchandise Mart in San Francisco, however, which soon resulted in a dwindling attendance of dealers at the Los Angeles shows. Eventually all of the furniture and floor covering tenants left and the building took on another identity—the Los Angeles Mart—serving the gift and accessory trade.

In 1975 FMAC again changed its name to the California Furniture Manufacturers Association (CFMA), and Leon J. Hahn became and served as executive vice president for the next 20 years until his retirement in 1985.

By 1978 the shareholders had grown older and less active in the business and were ready to sell their interests in the building when Richard Miller offered to buy them out. Henry Brandler, who had been a longtime board member of the Los Angeles Home Furnishings Mart, became president and manager of the Los Angeles Mart and in time would turn it into today's biggest and most successful permanent gift and accessory center in the West.

It had been an interesting and exciting journey filled with challenge and change, but it was far from being over. Lessons were learned, goals were defined, and the California furniture industry was headed in positive new directions.

*Above: Actor Rock Hudson was one of the many film celebrities who appeared at the Los Angeles Furniture Mart Home Furnishings Show in 1958. He is joined here by (clockwise from left) Henry Brandler, Eddy Feldman, Don Bates, Robert Mason, Richard Sax, Bud Toor, and Herman Kranz. Courtesy, Western Furnishings Manufacturers Association*

*Facing page: Escorted by her husband Mickey Hargitay, film legend Jayne Mansfield attended the gala black-tie event for the opening of the Home Furnishings Show in the fall of 1958. Courtesy, Western Furnishings Manufacturers Association*

# CHAPTER THREE

# THE CASE OF THE OPEN OR SHUT MARKET

## If You Can't Change Your Luck, Change Your Game. — Anonymous

In previous chapters, we have seen that due mainly to the pressures applied by retailers, who understandably didn't want suppliers, and freelance dealers, who had no stores or inventory, home furnishings marts traditionally were closed to everyone except legitimate dealers. And we know that all this would change. But before it did, some manufacturers tried to get around the restriction by opening showrooms in their factories, often on Saturdays, to sell to consumers. It wasn't well received and eventually would pretty much disappear.

Another, more dealer-acceptable avenue to the consumer market began to take shape in the years before World War II. Dealers opened wholesale showrooms, the forerunners of what are now usually known as "design centers," where clients are brought in by interior decorators and designers to see, touch, select, and buy the merchandise on display.

Eventually, all of the furniture marts and design centers would be both open and closed to one degree or another, influenced by the drastic shifts occurring in distribution. Even the High Point, North Carolina, mart, which is restricted to retailers during its market week, today allows designers and their clients in its showrooms the rest of the year.

The efforts to establish wholesale showrooms became more serious in the years following World War II. A number of furniture and decorative fabric representatives, for instance, grouped together to show their products in spaces located at 816 South Figueroa and on Santee Street. For awhile things went well, but in 1946 their landlords decided to double the rents, and a search for new quarters began.

Looking around carefully for the best possible sites, they came upon vacant land in an area that had already been discovered by Clark & Burchfield in 1945 for a decorative showroom. It consisted of property on La Cienega, Robertson, and Beverly boulevards, all within distance of the legendary and moneyed city of Beverly Hills. Subsequently, Albert Parvin & Company built an imposing showroom in 1948 on Robertson, near Clark & Burchfield's facility, and the following year bought a Herman Miller, Inc., showroom, conceived by renowned environmental designer Charles Eames, to Beverly Boulevard.

*In this photograph taken in 1958, Eddy Feldman, then managing director of the Los Angeles Furniture Mart, guides visitors through packed showroom floors during the Home Furnishings Show. This type of event was the forerunner of today's furniture marts and design centers, where decorators and designers bring their clients to select and purchase the merchandise on display. Courtesy, Western Furnishings Manufacturers Association*

*The latest technology in the furniture manufacturing business was featured at the 1962 Supply Show in the Los Angeles Sports Arena. Among the many booths and displays were Duraflake wood core products, Dacron polyester fiberfill by DuPont, and the staplers, tackers, and nailers by Western Duo-Fast. Courtesy, Western Furnishings Manufacturers Association*

Soon others would flock to the increasingly attractive area, including Knoll Associates; Martin Lowitz, an art dealer, who built a high-rise showroom office building; and Phyllis Morris, who manufactured the furniture she sold in her dramatic showroom. All were located on Beverly Boulevard. Towering over them was a spectacular 200,000-square-foot showroom building, known as Robertson Plaza, constructed in 1966. Today this building serves as headquarters for Pacific Theaters.

There is an interesting sidelight to the changes in distribution over the years that have made interior decorators and designers a mainstream pipeline to quality furniture and furnishings sales. The story recalls how in the 1960s, decorators and designers were forced to protect their involvement in the industry from competition that came from an unexpected quarter.

A number of opportunists had thought up a clever way to make money by enabling consumers to gain entrance into so-called closed showrooms. They conducted "schools" that supposedly taught interior design, and when the students paid their fees and completed the course, they were issued green cards. These cards were honored by many showrooms for admittance, and the sight of chauffeured limousines waiting outside while their wealthy green card owners completed furniture purchases inside, soon became common. This sight became increasingly worrisome to the genuine designers.

A concerted effort was quickly launched by the Los Angeles Chapter of the National Society of Interior Designers (now the American Society of Interior Designers) to end what they perceived as a serious threat to their

livelihood and professionalism.

Eventually the practice was halted, but not without consequences. Currently applicants must pass a grueling and extensive two-day examination before they can be accepted into the more than 60,000-member American Society of Interior Designers.

Paying close attention to all of the furniture showroom action going on around them were two realtors, Bert J. Friedman and Ronald S. Kates, who were familiar with the interior design business and whose own offices were at Beverly and Robertson boulevards. They knew that the opening of Cedars-Sinai Hospital had used up much of the available nearby land in the area and had also caused serious parking problems, developments that ended the idea of adding more showrooms in close proximity to each other.

Friedman and Kates came up with an idea: Why not create a major decorative arts center to bring showroom exhibitors together in one place? They approached the Southern Pacific Land Company (a subsidiary of Southern Pacific Railroad), which owned land at San Vicente and Melrose avenues, and made such a convincing presentation that Southern Pacific Land formed a partnership with Bircher Corporation and World Wide Group to plan and implement the project. In fact, Southern Pacific was so excited about the possibilities that famed architect Victor Gruen was retained to design the center.

The partnership turned the leasing and management of the Pacific Design Center (PDC) over to Friedman and Kates, who in 1971 hired Murray Feldman, a man whose background was encyclopedic in the furniture industry, ranging from designing to manufacturing and retailing, as

*Top: The early 1960s found the Modiline company to be a leading force in the manufacture of modern lighting fixtures. Courtesy, Western Furnishings Manufacturers Association*

*Bottom: The Suppliers Chapter, pictured here at the 1963 annual membership dinner, became an independent organization in the early 1980s after separating from the California Furniture Manufacturers Association in 1979. Now known as the Association of Western Furniture Suppliers, this group contracts directly with today's Western Furnishings Manufacturers Association. Courtesy, Western Furnishings Manufacturers Association*

*The first Pacific Design Center building, fondly known as the "Blue Whale," was completed in 1975 and offers 750,000 square feet of space in its impressive six-story structure. Photo by Larry Molmud*

well as working as marketing director.

In 1973 ground was broken for the huge, 750,000-square-foot, six-story blue Pacific Design Center (PDC), which would be known thereafter as the "Blue Whale." Completed in 1975, the Blue Whale was joined on the property by a second structure in 1987, a green eight-story, 425,000-square-foot building, called the "Emerald City." Another building is in the planning stage; it will be covered in maroon glass and used as a meeting center and hotel. Together the PDC buildings direct their principal efforts toward furnishing the contract businesses such as hotels, motels, and offices, although some residential furniture, mostly top of the line, is shown.

Murray Feldman, who contributed so much to the furniture industry, died in late 1987 and is remembered today by The Murray Feldman Gallery, a free-standing structure in a plaza between the Blue Whale and Emerald City. The gallery is used for various industry exhibitions since its dedication in the spring of 1988 during PDC's annual West Week.

West Week is an innovative four-day event that attracts leading designers, architects, futurists, scientists, planners, and others; it is often the forum for the introduction of new designs. As a consequence of earlier efforts by Feldman, the already existing showrooms in the Beverly and Robertson boulevards area joined with the Pacific Design Center to make West Week a coordinated area market week. This merger resulted in the West Hollywood and Los Angeles districts becoming known as the "Avenues of Design."

After the Los Angeles Furniture Mart building was sold and became the Los Angeles mart in 1978, Ragnar C. Qvale, a prominent Los Angeles archi-

tect, and his brother, Szell Qvale of San Francisco, saw an opportunity to provide showroom facilities for the manufacturers and furniture representatives who had been displaced. They purchased the Title Insurance and Trust Building, an art deco landmark at 433 South Spring Street, from Southern Pacific Railroad and remodeled it into the Design Center of Los Angeles, complete with a fine restaurant on the top floor.

Both the building and the idea were excellent and worked well for a time, but unfortunately the area became increasingly run down. Retailers and designers soon had no desire to venture there. A real estate syndicate, however, viewed the future of the location from a different perspective, and in December 1988 bought the handsome old building from the Qvale brothers. The real estate group leased it to the Los Angeles City Central Library as its main facility because the library had recently suffered major fire damage.

In addition to the Blue Whale, the Emerald City, and the individual Beverly and Robertson area showrooms, there are several other noteworthy operations in Southern California. The Los Angeles Mart at 1933 South Broadway, devotes four floors to what has been described as probably the country's finest collection of commercial and residential furniture. The mart also sells gifts and accessories. These showrooms are owned by manufacturers' representatives and individuals other than manufacturers.

The Bircher Corporation, which owns part of the Blue Whale, has two showrooms, Design Center South in Laguna Niguel and another in San Diego. Most of their tenants display residential furniture and many of them also maintain showrooms at the Pacific Design Center.

San Francisco, which still is home to a number of furniture manufacturers, has Showplace Square, which features open and closed showrooms primarily for the interior design trade, and the San Francisco Furniture Market Center, formerly known as the Western Merchandise Mart.

The development of furniture marts and showrooms has brought the furniture industry a long way from those early times when the only way manufacturers' representatives could reach their customers was by traveling their territories on bicycles, streetcars, and trains and, in later years, in buses and automobiles. Obviously unable to carry furniture with them, they had to depend on photographs and drawings in catalogues, along

*Above: The Western Furniture Mart showroom floor (now named the San Francisco Furniture Market Center) featured a vast selection of modern designs in the 1940s. Courtesy, Western Furnishings Manufacturers Association*

*Below: Located at 1933 South Broadway in downtown Los Angeles, the Los Angeles Mart boasts four floors of fine commercial and residential furniture. Photo by Larry Molmud*

*The new Furniture Manufacturers Association of California officers for 1968 were officially recognized at the installation ceremonies during the group's convention of that same year. Pictured from left to right are, Lee Hahn, executive director; Joe Inco, president; Peter Funston, treasurer; Bob Blumenthal, vice president; and Quirino Furiani, secretary. Courtesy, Bob Blumenthal*

with samples of finishes and upholstery fabrics.

In the 1870s, efforts were made to solve that problem. Some furniture manufacturers decided to reach the consumer directly by showing actual product samples in rented spaces in large metropolitan areas such as New York. The first real breakthrough was made by Grand Rapids factories when they took part in the 1878 Centennial Philadelphia Exhibition. So successful was the experience that retailers and designers were soon flocking to Grand Rapids looking for new furniture lines. The manufacturers were ecstatic and began showing their merchandise wherever they could find space: in their own factories, hotel lobbies and mezzanines, even in rented store fronts.

One major result of that productive method of marketing was the founding of the nation's first multi-occupancy furniture market building in Grand Rapids in 1889 by Delos A. Blodgett. Philip J. Klingman, a sharp-eyed and successful manufacturers' representative, immediately rented two floors from Blodgett for his lines, and business was so good that it was not long before he took on a partner and leased the entire building.

Although other entrepreneurs soon seized on the idea and opened exhibit operations in Grand Rapids to attract manufacturers from other areas of the country, the problem of not having a permanent, coordinated industry furniture mart arose, the same dilemma that would plague Southern California manufacturers later. But Grand Rapids, unlike southern and northern California, never did succeed in establishing the equivalent of a Los Angeles

*Above: Babyline stepped in to fill the post-war need for baby furniture, manufacturing cribs and changing tables just as fast as Southern Californians were manufacturing babies. Note the women to the right painting details on crib parts by hand. Courtesy, Western Furnishings Manufacturers Association*

*Below: Actor William Bendix (left) hammed it up with Mr. Jacobs, (right) president of Babyline products, to demonstrate the sturdy construction of this fine nursery furniture. Courtesy, Western Furnishings Manufacturers Association*

Furniture Mart or a San Francisco Western Merchandise Mart.

Vast changes have also taken place in the way furniture is distributed and marketed to the public. In the old days, independent retail stores were the principal outlets for manufacturers and, of course, some continue to operate using a personal service, hands-on style, usually selling top-of-the-line furniture through interior designers. In fact, small entrepreneurial retail stores and manufacturers, who sell and make specialized types of furniture, are appearing again in some strength. But the big change is in midlevel-quality furniture, sold at competitive retail prices by huge chains with powerful advertising campaigns and the advantage of volume-purchase discounts from manufacturers.

Another development that has had a major impact on the furniture industry is called "KD" or knockdown wood furniture. (Knockdown furniture refers to furniture that can easily be assembled or disassembled.) Accounting for much of the furniture sold in America today, it is manufactured under contract in such places as Hong Kong, Taiwan, and Bangkok from lumber grown in the United States. Knockdown furniture is then shipped back to this country in space-saving cartons to be assembled locally by American firms that don't own factories or actually make furniture. A side effect of this high-volume business on U.S. furniture manufacturers has been the creation of a shortage of such popular woods as alder, along with hefty price increases on what is available.

Former FMASC president Percy Solotoy points out another reason why knockdown furniture has been able to so successfully invade the market. When World War II ended, countries such as Taiwan had no furniture factories. Later when factories were built, Taiwan imported engineers from Germany to design and install the newest and most advanced computerized technology and equipment available.

California manufacturers, on the other hand, generally own factories that have been in existence for years and they cannot afford to duplicate the state-of-the-art facilities of the Orient, making it difficult to compete with such innovations as KD furniture. These manufacturers own small operations, most employing fewer

*The mill in the Brown-Saltman factory, shown here in the 1960s, was arranged in an efficient horseshoe pattern, enabling the workers to take advantage of natural light from the windows. The milled parts were then sent to the factory's assembly room. Courtesy, Western Furnishings Manufacturers Association*

than 100 people, while the average Taiwan plant can have as many as 1,000 workers.

There is no implication that Southern California furniture makers are imperiled, for they actually are in a fast-growing industry, but one which is growing differently than before and is changing in its nature and direction.

For example, the large furniture plants located in High Point, North Carolina, mostly owned by huge conglomerates, will continue as production operations, while the smaller entrepreneurial factories in Southern California will survive and prosper by concentrating on becoming producers of custom or semi-custom furniture.

There has also been enormous growth in the commercial furniture manufacturing area, supplying metal chairs, desks, filing cabinets, and other office equipment to the rapidly expanding market of new and expanding businesses.

Although California manufacturers have had to defer to the Orient in terms of completely modern factories, the very first furniture production line actually was developed in Los Angeles by David Saltman of Brown-Saltman, located at the time in a huge building, a former brewery, located on Main Street.

Saltman conceived the idea of a metal cart that had stringers on which a wood furniture frame could be placed; bins on each side of the cart held such things as springs, tacks, and filling materials. Mounted on wheels, it was pushed manually from one station to the next until the piece of furniture was completed and deposited in the shipping department. The ingenious system enabled them to produce 103 upholstered three-piece sets (sofa, chair, and small chair) per day. Later, it would be copied by residential and commercial manufacturers, and improved upon by setting the cart on a chain instead of wheels. In this way the movement was automated, although the system was designed to stop so that the furniture could be removed and worked on at each step.

Other innovative furniture manufacturing ideas sometimes came from unexpected places, such as the automobile industry.

Prior to the early 1950s the furniture industry, both manufacturers and re-

*David Saltman of the Brown-Saltman Furniture Manufacturing Company, whose factory is shown here in 1963, developed the first furniture production line, creating a new wave of manufacturing for the furniture industry. This breakthrough enabled the company to produce 103 three-piece sets each business day. Courtesy, Western Furnishings Manufacturers Association*

tailers, relied on and were limited to the skills of an upholsterer. The upholsterer, more commonly referred to as a "tack spitter," would place sterilized tacks into his mouth, using his tongue to work each one headfirst onto a magnetic tack hammer. This process eliminated wasted handmotion and gave him great speed. While he drove a tack home into the piece, he was already moving the next one into place with his tongue. One retired Los Angeles manufacturer recalls that when he was a 10-year-old schoolboy, his job was to sweep up all the dropped tacks from the floor after the upholsterers had gone home. Then he threw them back into the barrel to be used again, which presumably negated the sterilization.

These craftsmen were superior workers, but difficult to train or replace and long apprenticeships were required. Then air-driven staplers were invented in 1948 to attach fabric to the interior shell of automobiles, and the tack spitters' days were numbered. The inventor, Al Juilf, and two partners formed a new firm, Senco Products, Inc., and set about trying to convince the furniture manufacturers to replace the tack spitters with the new pneumatic tool. A proud lot, the tack spitters resisted mightily, but the factory owners quickly saw the time-saving benefits that could be made without any loss of quality. Later on, larger and more powerful tools would be developed, which today are used at nearly every workstation in the furniture assembly plant.

In 1960 an idea was considered, fleetingly, to stamp the date of manufacture somewhere reasonably visible on each piece of furniture. The thought was that people would replace their furniture with newer models, just like in the automotive industry, if they could be reminded how old it was. Fortunately, wiser heads prevailed.

California was—and still is—noted for its ability to often be the first to introduce new concepts to the nation and the world, some outlandish or splashy or short-lived, but many concepts possess merit, good taste, and lasting qualities. One of the successful concepts is California furniture design, which as we shall see, has earned its own special place in the "golden odyssey" of the industry in the state.

# CHAPTER FOUR

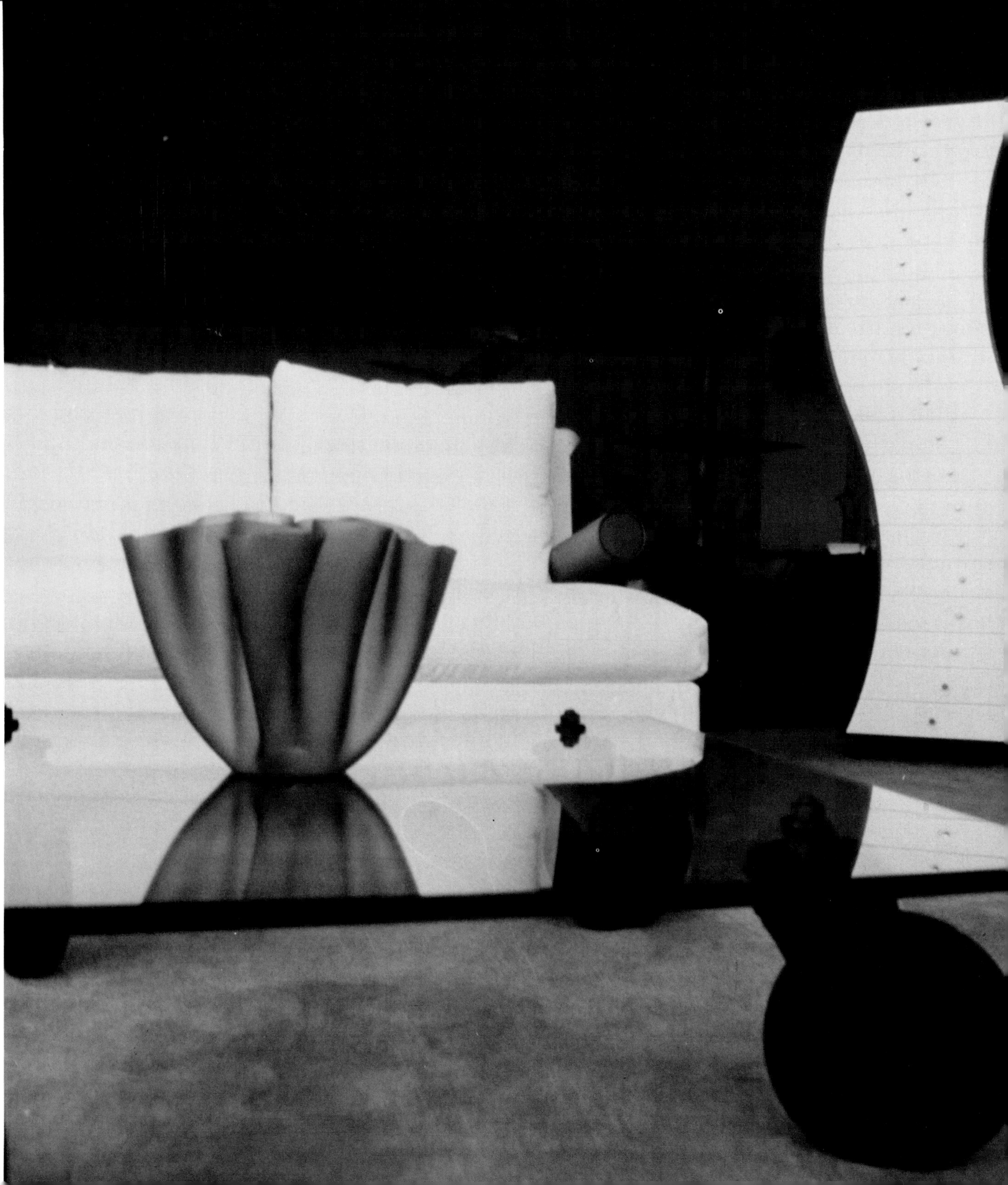

# THE CALIFORNIA LOOK AND MURPHY'S BED

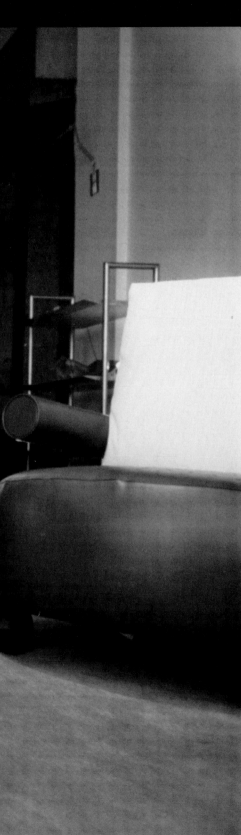

## Originality Is Not Necessarily Better Than Imitation, But It Makes Imitation Possible. — Anonymous

Architectural designs and furniture styles are living arts influenced by and reflecting the ever-shifting social, economic, cultural, and technological changes and advances of society. They often borrow from the best of the past, giving a sense of continuity, but they also create new contemporary shapes and patterns that become the links to the future. In that way, they are an integral and expressive part of our lives that go beyond mere necessity or function.

Perhaps nowhere is the truth of that more evident than in the history of furniture design in California.

Perched on the farthermost rim of the continental United States, California's geographic distance from the major trendsetting centers of the western world has never stopped it from developing all kinds of original ideas and products that people everywhere frequently adapt or adopt.

The ability to influence tastes and life-styles of others has become something of a trademark for a place that many outsiders regard, perhaps not wholly inaccurately, as more of a state of mind than a state, which perhaps is a part of its irresistible charm.

Take "the California Look," for example, a term that describes a design that not only uniquely reflects its source, but propelled the Golden State's furniture industry onto the international stage after World War II.

The California Look was, and is, an imprecise design, in that there are no real boundaries on how it is interpreted. What makes it clearly recognizable, however, is the way it communicates a feeling for the informality of the casual indoor and outdoor California life-style, a sense that is accented by the profuse use of color in fabrics and finishes and the emphasis on comfort.

Before the California Look riveted the world's attention on California-made furniture in the 1940s, the state's design influence in the industry was minimal at best. Prior to World War I, most of the product design was copied by local production manufacturers from other producers in the East and elsewhere. Perhaps because their market was limited to the western region, there wasn't much incentive for them to do otherwise. A little original design work was being done, mostly by individual craftsmen and archi-

*Furniture displays around Beverly and La Cienega boulevards in Los Angeles feature a wide selection of furniture styles, from classic antiques to these playful modern pieces—designs that capture the essence of the ever-popular "California" style. Photo by Jonathan Nourok*

*Right: California's furniture industry was thrust into the international spotlight after World War II with the introduction of the exciting new "California Look," and many of the women who were employed during the war stayed on to help fill the growing needs of this booming market. Courtesy, Western Furnishings Manufacturers Association*

*Below: Los Angeles furniture manufacturer Stockwell-Kling featured the California Bungalow line in one of its early catalogs, referring to it as a "typical 'California' design." Delicately finished in enamel, this suite of furniture was striped and decorated with decalcomania transfers. Courtesy, Western Furnishings Manufacturers Association*

tects, and although some of it achieved wide attention, none of it was ever mass-produced.

Notable among those few early California designers were Charles Sumner Greene (1868-1957) and his brother, Henry M. Greene (1870-1954), whose work can still be found in homes they built in Pasadena.

Their furniture designs, which were made into finished pieces by Peter and John Hall of Pasadena, showed some influence derived from the early Franciscan missionaries. Charles Greene was taken with the work of the Spanish friars, making the following comments in 1905.

*The old art of California—that of the mission fathers—is old enough to be romantic and mysterious enough too. Study it and you will find a deeper meaning than books tell of, or sun-dried bricks and plaster show. Then, too, those old monks came from a climate not unlike this [and] built after their own fashion . . . Therefore, giving heed to those necessary and effective qualities there is good and just reason why we should study their works . . .*

Other designers of that time include Arthur and Lewis Mathews in northern California, who created what became known as the California Decorative Style.

As dean of the Mark Hopkins Institute in San Francisco, Arthur met a young woman student, Lucia Kleinhans, who was attending the institute's School of Design.

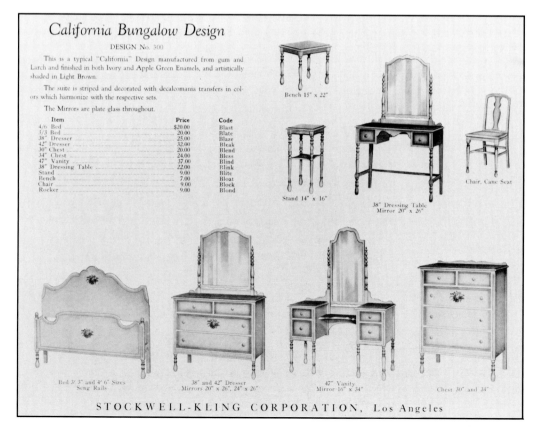

## California Bungalow Design

DESIGN No. 300

This is a typical "California" Design manufactured from gum and Larch and finished in both Ivory and Apple Green Enamels, and artistically shaded in Light Brown.

The suite is striped and decorated with decalcomania transfers in colors which harmonize with the respective sets.

The Mirrors are plate glass throughout.

| Item | Price | Code |
|---|---|---|
| 4/6 Bed | $20.00 | Blast |
| 3/3 Bed | 20.00 | Blate |
| 38" Dresser | 25.00 | Blaze |
| 42" Dresser | 32.00 | Bleak |
| 30" Chest | 20.00 | Blend |
| 34" Chest | 24.00 | Bless |
| 47" Vanity | 37.00 | Blind |
| 38" Dressing Table | 22.00 | Blink |
| Stand | 9.00 | Blite |
| Bench | 7.00 | Bloat |
| Chair | 9.00 | Block |
| Rocker | 9.00 | Blond |

Bench 15" x 22"

Stand 14" x 16"

38" Dressing Table
Mirror 20" x 26"

Chair, Cane Seat

Bed 3' 3" and 4' 6" Sizes
Seng Rails

38" and 42" Dresser
Mirrors 20" x 26", 24" x 26"

47" Vanity
Mirror 16" x 34"

Chest 30" and 34"

STOCKWELL-KLING CORPORATION, Los Angeles

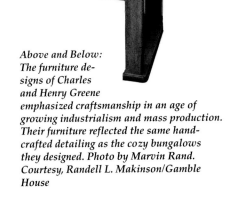

Eventually they married and opened the Furniture Shop in 1906, designing and producing handsome pieces for both residential and contract customers. Although they had begun business in the very year of San Francisco's devastating earthquake and fire, their only aftershock was the way their business boomed during the rebuilding of the city.

California furniture designers generally trained somewhere else, perhaps in Europe or in the eastern or southern United States. There was no formal program in California to teach the art of furniture design until 1950, when the Art Center School in Los Angeles decided that the industry was well enough established to support the students it planned to graduate.

The Art Center School had been founded in 1930 by Edward A. Adams to teach product design—mostly automotive—and graphic arts. The school hired John Keal, the most active top designer in the state and a former UCLA extension course teacher in furniture design, to teach the course as an upper division major.

The new program even attracted a scholarship, the David J. Saltman Scholarship in Furniture Design, and students were recruited. Over the next three years, designers graduated, but industry did not or could not absorb the new professionals and the program was dropped.

Influenced by avant garde architects and designers

*Above and Below: The furniture designs of Charles and Henry Greene emphasized craftsmanship in an age of growing industrialism and mass production. Their furniture reflected the same hand-crafted detailing as the cozy bungalows they designed. Photo by Marvin Rand. Courtesy, Randell L. Makinson/Gamble House*

in Europe, the U.S. furniture industry slowly and warily began to venture beyond the tried-and-true boundaries of traditional design into new, unexplored, and exciting areas of modernity early in the 1900s.

Just as the movement was beginning to get somewhere in America, the country suddenly was flooded with imported reproductions of French, eighteenth-century English, Spanish Tudor, and Italian antique furniture that had become tremendously popular almost overnight.

It was an ironic twist: Old Europe was going crazy for the new Bauhaus or "design for use" approach that recognized the need to accommodate modern innovations and life-styles, while America was reaching romantically into the dusty memories of the past.

As a result of that invasion in 1920, U.S. designers were largely pushed aside and would not return until 1925, when the scarcity of their work was noticed by manufacturers, retailers, and consumers attending the Paris Exhibition of Arts.

That concern was quickly translated into a new and vigorous rebirth of modern styles. Architects such as Frank Lloyd Wright led the way with novel concepts of unifying space and form in the houses and furniture he designed.

At first, American furniture manufacturers approached the changeover cautiously, remembering that such styles as "l'art nouveau" and "art deco" had never become runaway bestsellers. But a few Californian producers jumped in enthusiastically and "art moderne" soon began to fill retail floors and decorator showrooms.

Brown-Saltman Furniture Manufacturing Company in Los Angeles was the industry's most daring and innovative leader of the new movement, hiring such famous designers as Paul Theodore Frankl, that "incorrigible modernist" whose call to arms was "No compromise with tradition!," and Paul Laszlo. Frankl, who had emigrated to the United States from Germany, became well-known for his "sky-scraper" furniture, including tall bookcases and cabinets and long, deep, comfortable upholstered pieces. Laszlo, a Hungarian, earned a respected name for such projects as his remodeling of several departments in Bullock's Wilshire department store and the interiors and furniture of a number of rooms in the Beverly Hills Hotel. A couple of furniture lines were also designed for Brown-Saltman by Gilbert Rodhe (1894-1944), whose fame stemmed mainly from his work for Herman Miller, Inc.

Another California designer who influenced art moderne in its early days

# Art Moderne—

## BECOMES A LIVABLE FASHION

*The cool, intellectual aloofness of the room at right soothes fretted nerves and offers quiet comfort to a weary body. A very livable interpretation of Art Moderne*

YOU will see many freakish things committed in the name of Art Moderne — faddish things that will live only for a moment. They are not the true Art Moderne. The new creations of really great furniture designers are as livable and comfortable and satisfying as anything that has gone before. Glance at the rooms shown here. Different, yes! But satisfying, aren't they? Simplicity, practicality and comfort combine in a new and very livable beauty. Soft neutral colors rest the spirit, and clean, straight-to-the-point lines give evidence of practical twentieth century directness.

*It is interesting to note the subtle neutral colors many of the modernists have adopted—schemes in pale beige, ivory, silver, grey and white—as contrasted with the startling combinations others affect.*

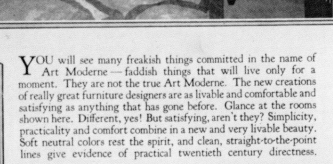

*Nothing startling about the room above. Modern furniture like this fits in almost any home and mingles sociably with furniture of many other periods.*

*Modernists discover many amusing ways to make every inch of space count for something. The ends of the davenport at right serve as book cases.*

*A modernistic wall paper is used in the bedroom above. Such a design might prove disquieting after a while, but it is undeniably interesting. Note the sleek low dressing table and the wing chair with bizarre covering.*

*Right: Paul Theodore Frankl was a leading force in the new Art Moderne movement of the 1920s and 1930s. This captivating dining room set is indicative of his engaging and innovative style. Courtesy, Western Furnishings Manufacturers Association*

*Below: Designer Gilbert Rodhe created this stunning bedroom ensemble for Brown-Saltman in 1938, and was also extremely well-known for his work with Herman Miller, Inc. Courtesy, Western Furnishings Manufacturers Association*

*Facing page: Featuring some 750,000 square feet of space, the six-story blue Pacific Design Center was soon joined by a second building of green glass, which boasts eight floors and 450,000 square feet. Affectionately known as the "Blue Whale" and the "Emerald City," respectively, these majestic structures will soon have a third addition made of maroon glass, which will be used as a meeting center and hotel. Photo by Larry Molmud*

was Kem Weber, who owned retail furniture stores in Santa Barbara and Berkeley, and for several years was director of the decorating and furnishings department at Barker Bros., a top furniture dealer. Although Weber's designs apparently were never mass-produced in California, his custom pieces were popular and examples of his work can be found today in museums.

Weber felt the industry should exclusively use art moderne design. In a report published in *Furniture West* in 1933, he didn't mince words.

*Present designs are not adapted to present day methods of construction,"* he said. *"For example, as long as we use imitation candles for electric illumination, we haven't understood the essence of electric illumination; the same is true of the various types of period furniture that are in use today, Monterey, Louis XIV, etc.*

"No one would think of driving around in a coach and four today," he triumphantly concluded. "Why, then should people use furniture design from another day and age?"

For a time the industry sucessfully used modern design, but World War II brought it to an abrupt end. Most of California's major furniture factories became involved in military procurement work and the few plants that continued to produce for the pinched consumer market had no need to worry about introducing new designs to help sell their product.

After the war, California attracted a huge influx of people from the East and Midwest, many seeking and finding jobs as industries rushed to con-

*Left: Furniture manufacturing in California has come a long way since the early days of the industry when all pieces were individually hand-crafted. Today's state-of-the-art technology, such as this paint assembly line at the Alu Mont Furniture facility in Irwindale, affords fine quality workmanship for a reasonable cost. Photo by Jonathan Nourok*

*Right: Huipio Conrado puts the finishing touches on a barstool base at Mikhail Darafeev, Inc., a Baldwin Park firm specializing in game room furniture. Photo by Jonathan Nourok*

*Left: The Alu Mont Furniture Manufacturing Corporation in Irwindale features a wide array of aluminum furniture. Here, employee Zenobio Delgadillo polishes an assortment of table bases at the corporation's facility. Photo by Jonathan Nourok*

*Above: The more than 500,000 square feet of space at the Harper's facility in Torrance houses the company's corporate headquarters, showrooms, and manufacturing facilities, part of which is shown here. Photo by Jonathan Nourok*

*Left: The breakthrough technology of computer aided design has helped to establish great strides in the modern-day manufacture of furniture in California. Designer Ron Storf is shown here in the process of drawing plans for a chair base at the Harper's facility in Los Angeles. Photo by Jonathan Nourok*

*Left: Even the architectural details of the West Hollywood area design and furniture shops highlight the ever-popular and elusive "California" style. Photo by Jonathan Nourok*

*Below: Trendy Melrose Avenue near the Pacific Design Center is lined with stores and services that cater to the specific needs of the design trade. Photo by Jonathan Nourok*

# CLASSIC

*Above: The traditional art of fashioning wicker furniture has been revived on Melrose Avenue, where classic designs meet contemporary tastes. Photo by Jonathan Nourok*

*Facing page photos: Contemporary Beverly Boulevard is reflected in the window of Diva, a store specializing in the most whimsical and modern examples of California design. Passersby stop to gaze at the captivating window designs during a Sunday afternoon stroll. Photos by Jonathan Nourok*

*Right: West Hollywood is home to the "Creative City," where furniture showrooms and other fine interior design resources can be found in the vicinity of Melrose Avenue and Beverly, Robertson, and La Cienega boulevards. Photo by Jonathan Nourok*

vert back to the production of peacetime consumer goods. These new immigrants bought or built homes, creating a real estate and furnishings boom almost everywhere.

The state's furniture industry began making progress again, although its perennial problems continued. These included a lack of adequate supplies of locally produced raw materials such as lumber, hardware, and fabrics; relatively high labor costs; and the great distances to consumer markets outside of California. The combined problems contributed to a distinct price disadvantage for those on the West Coast in their competition with midwestern, eastern, and southern manufacturers. Price disadvantages affected them even in their own state, which is still true today.

What compensated for those obstacles was the development of the marvelous California Look, that ubiquitous style that gave impetus to the furnishings industry. Most of the professional designers who helped develop the California Look lived in California and understood and appreciated the environment they were interpreting. The list is too long to repeat here, but it was those talented people who made possible the tremendous resurgence and growth of the industry at a time when something spectacular was needed to prevent it from stagnating.

The California Look brought retailers flooding to the furniture marts in San Francisco and Los Angeles, eager to see and buy the new product. The innovative furniture style even went "on the road," traveling to the Merchandise Mart in Chicago to bring the message to midwestern, eastern, and southern dealers. That venture was arranged by such leading California manufacturers as Brown-Saltman, Crown Upholstery Company, Sherman/Bertram Company, Cal Mode Furniture Manufacturing Company, Furniture Guild of California, Glenn of California, and Morris Furniture Manufacturing Company.

Grouped together in Chicago's mart, the suppliers called their display area "The California Corridor," which would continue to exist for a few years until different versions of the California Look and other new designs began to appear in manufacturers' lines nationwide, and retailers no longer were restricted to the West in their search for fresh and innovative pieces.

Because the California Look was more the interpretation of an idea rather than a specific design, anyone could copy or modify it. Often that meant some of California's small, entrepreneurial manufacturers, who could not afford their own designers, would resort to copying the creative ideas of other suppliers.

*Facing page: Now the central branch of the Los Angeles Public Library, the stately Art Deco landmark at 433 South Spring Street in downtown Los Angeles once housed the Design Center of Los Angeles. Photo by Larry Molmud*

*Above: California furniture manufacturers reflected the California lifestyle in their innovative designs and their imaginative advertising campaigns. This creative ad depicts the California lifestyle taken to its ultimate fulfillment. Courtesy, Security Pacific National Bank Photographic Collection/Los Angeles Public Library*

*Right: Enticements of all types were used for attracting buyers to furniture marts and showrooms displaying the incredibly popular California design in the 1960s. Pictured here in front of the Los Angeles Furniture Mart advertising the new Winter Home Furnishings Market, from left to right are Herman Kranz, vice president of the Furniture Manufacturers Association of California, an unidentified model, and Eddy S. Feldman, executive secretary of the association. Courtesy, Western Furnishings Manufacturers Association*

*From the craze of the Monterey-style furniture in the 1920s to the modern sets of today's box office hits, the Hollywood film industry has truly inspired many memorable California furniture designs. Courtesy, California Historical Society, San Francisco*

Copying ideas was an old problem that reached back to the beginning of the century and one which even today has not been totally resolved. This problem really began right after World War I, when for some unrecorded reason an arbitrary decision was made to hold two markets a year at which manufacturers would display their products to retail dealers. Factories were expected to bring forth new styles at each show, a tough challenge even for the larger manufacturers who could afford either in-house or freelance designers.

Predictably, imitators sprang up right and left, often encouraged by unprincipled retailers who showed them the latest designs created by others. The imitators would then manufacture and sell the finished pieces to retailers at low cost. Inevitably, the industry suffered as the product and its prices were cheapened in that fashion.

A word was coined that described generally showy pieces that appeared well crafted, but were shoddily made. This word also described high pressure marketing tactics used to sell the copies to the public. The word was "borax," a slang term derived from the time when borax soap manufacturers offered cheap furniture as coupon premiums.

In 1919, reputable furniture suppliers became so incensed by the activities of the design copiers that they took their case to the newly formed Furniture Manufacturers Association in Los Angeles.

A self-policing system was set up, which required each member to provide FMA with photographs of all their "active patterns." The idea, of course, was to eliminate the possibility of "two or more members of the Association making the same design."

Going a step further, the FMA also decided to instruct members, who were planning to bring out new patterns, to check with each other so that

*Architect and designer R.M. Schindler designed furniture that functioned as an extension of his homes. This design for the Oliver home in Los Angeles, shown here in 1934, combines couch, table, and bookcases in one multi-level extension of the fireplace. Courtesy, Security Pacific National Bank Photographic Collection/Los Angeles Public Library*

there would be no duplication. But the procedure for resolving disputes was not established until 1921. "Should members fail to agree, the matter shall be referred to a disinterested committee of five, appointed by the Executive Committee of FMA, who will meet with the members and make such recommendations as will eliminate the duplication and it shall be the duty of both sides to accept the Committee's decision as final and abide by its recommendations."

In an attempt to head off such possible confrontations, the FMA instructed in its longwinded document that

*Any member planning NEW DESIGNS must immediately notify the Secretary of his intention to produce same, at the same time furnishing drawings, specifications and proposed sale price, if possible, before proceeding with the manufacture and marketing of same, so that he may decide whether design conflicts with any patterns now on file, or duplicates new specifications which have been filed but not yet placed on the market.* Then finally, "If the Secretary decides it is a duplication of another member's pattern, the matter shall be referred to the Special Committee of Five for final judgment."

It was a noble effort, but doomed from the start. There was absolutely no way in which the Committee of Five or anyone else could successfully enforce the rules.

Over the years, other attempts would be made by the industry to control the problem of pattern duplication, but without much success. About the only route open to protect creators of original furniture today is design patents, but if there is litigation it can be expensive and so lengthy that by the time a case is resolved, the pattern in question is unlikely to even be on the market.

Sometimes adapting a design idea from outside the industry can result in a whole new popular line of furniture. That's what happened in 1927 when Hollywood set furniture patterned on the Monterey style was created for a movie named *Arizona.* Some buyers for Barker Bros. saw the film and although what they felt about the picture is not recorded, it is known that

they thought the furniture was terrific. They got their hands on a still photo from the film and took it to Frank Mason of Mason Furniture Manufacturing Company, telling him that there was great potential for a line of similarly styled pieces. Mason agreed and had his son, George, redesign the movie set furniture for production and put it on the market.

Mason's "Monterey" furniture can only be described as a box office bonanza, sweeping the country like a stampeding herd in a cowboy movie. Indeed, a measure of its long-lived popularity is that Mason was still selling it in 1947. Soon after it appeared others would imitate, including Jaeger Furniture Manufacturing Company and Brown-Saltman Furniture Manufacturing Company, which brought out its own highly successful Monterey-style "Ease-A-Way" chair.

*The Murphy-In-A-Door Beds were welcome additions for cramped apartment dwellers in the early 1900s when space was at a premium. This space-saving design soon appeared throughout most small city apartments and eventually found its way into the popular slapstick comedy films of the day. These beds were not only convenient and comfortable, their comic potential was endless. Courtesy, Security Pacific National Bank Photographic Collection/Los Angeles Public Library*

Later, in the mid-1940s, Brown-Saltman experienced a different kind of connection with Hollywood. For several years, a sample of every single piece of furniture they made was bought by Universal Studios' set designer for use in movies. In the end, Universal owned the best collection of Brown-Saltman furniture in the world.

One type of furniture introduced in the early 1930s was "built-ins," designed by such Los Angeles architects as Vienna-born R.M. Schindler. His idea was to make it "impossible to tell where the house ends and the furniture begins." Not only that, but the furniture could be "built easily by the carpenter on the job rather than by a cabinetmaker." It was the kind of development that could make furniture producers, designers, and dealers break out in a cold sweat during the night, but it never caught on.

One built-in that prospered, however, though it was never a threat to the industry, was the famous "Murphy-In-A-Door Bed." Back in 1900, most apartments in California were short on space and no one knew that better than inventor William L. Murphy in his one-room San Francisco flat. The story goes that in addition to needing more space than he had, he worried that young lady visitors might misunderstand his intentions if they saw a bed sitting in the middle of the room. So he invented a mechanism that made it possible to swing a bed up into a cabinet or an opening in the wall behind it.

It was a clever idea and became so popular through the years that a U.S. Court of Appeals has ruled that the term "Murphy Bed" is now a part of the language and even the inventor's descendants cannot register it as their private trademark.

Other imaginative furniture ideas that were born in California include the water bed, which was considered a "hippie" item until mainstream dealers began to offer them and landlords were told by the California legislature they could not turn away water-bed-owning tenants if they carried insurance against possible damage.

Paper furniture was another novelty that turned up in 1968 in the form of tables and chairs designed in pressed cardboard by Jerry Johnson and Jack Griner and made by Plywood Benders, Inc. Later, internationally known architect Frank Gehry would introduce an extensive line of the unusual furniture.

*Facing page and left: Architect Frank O. Gehry first designed cardboard furniture in the early 1970s, selling his pieces for $100 at Bloomingdales. These pieces have now become collector's items worth thousands of dollars. Gehry ventured back into cardboard furniture design in the 1980s and two of his recent works are shown here. Courtesy, Frank O. Gehry & Associates*

Several multipurpose and space-saving furniture designs also originated in the Golden State. One Los Angeles manufacturer of fine mahogany furniture in 1924 was offering a hutch that could be used with table and chairs in the living room. Others included sofa-beds and duo-beds connected by a center table, reclining chairs for sitting and sleeping, drop leaf tables for dining or decoration, and sofas with radios in the arms. Somehow it seems appropriate that such interesting and often useful novelties are the inventive product of California.

The history of furniture design in California is rich with creativity and originality. Even in today's fiercely competitive and diversified marketplace, the industry continues to have a profound influence on the world's tastes; nowhere perhaps is this more consistently noticeable as in its stylish, colorful, comfortable, and technologically advanced California outdoor furniture.

A good example of how that momentum is sustained was an event put on by a group of manufacturers in the Los Angeles Furniture Mart in 1975. Called "California Lifestyles . . . An Experience in Living," it was an effort to draw attention to the uniqueness of California design in much the same way as the highly successful California Look had done.

Although it did not recreate the tremendous nationwide market excitement of those earlier years, what it did achieve was to send an important reminder to the nation's interior designers, retailers, and the public to keep their eyes on the West Coast as an important source of new and exciting ideas.

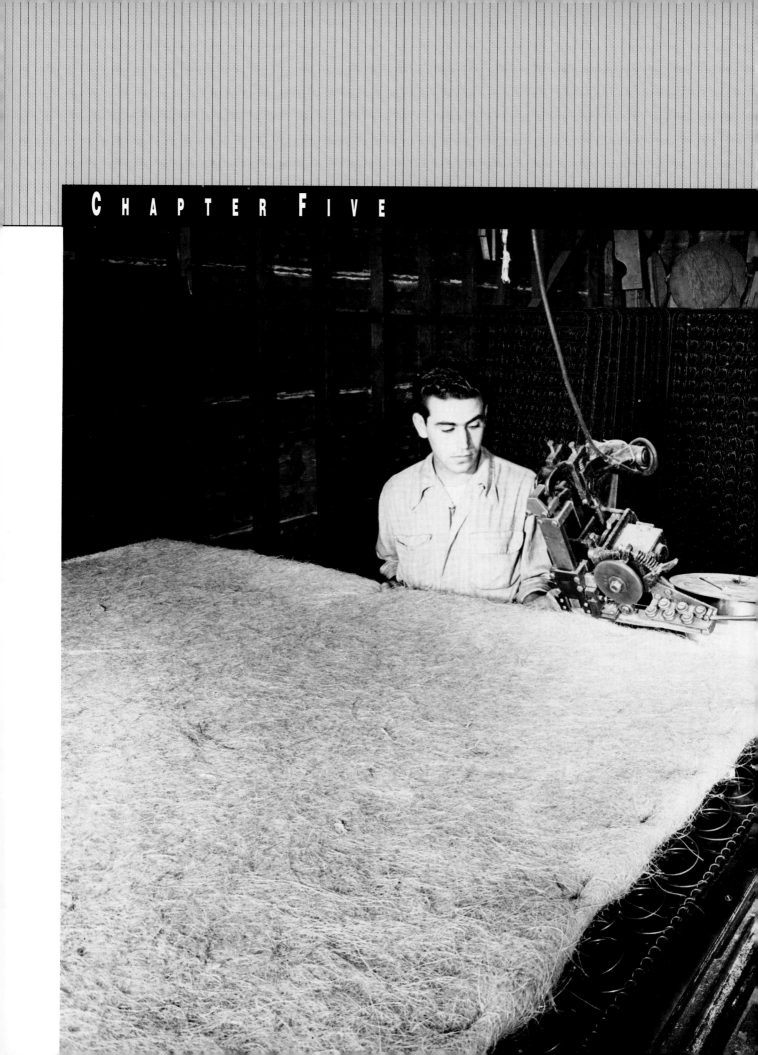

# THIS TAG MUST NOT BE REMOVED

## What You Don't Know Can Hurt You.
### — Anonymous

A history of the California furniture industry would be incomplete without including its unique leadership role in the development of public health and safety manufacturing standards, a fascinating but little-known story of major proportions in terms of its far-reaching impact inside and outside the state.

Surely there are few people who haven't felt at least a twinge of uneasiness when cutting off the information tag attached to upholstered furniture, cushions, pillows, and mattresses they have bought. "Under penalty of law, this tag must not be removed" is the stern warning. Even though it should be obvious that this part of the message is not directed to consumers, but rather to retailers, many don't continue to read the rest of the wording; the tag describes the materials used to make and fill the cover, as well as how the piece meets flammability and other safety and health regulations. These requirements did not exist in California or anywhere else prior to 1909.

Before laws were passed to protect the consumer, manufacturers were under no restrictions as to the kinds of materials they used or how sanitary or safe they were. Short of cutting open the cover or fabric to find out what really lay beneath, the user was completely at the mercy of the producer, some of whom were often less than honest.

The list of materials used to stuff bedding and furniture to make sleeping and sitting more comfortable is almost unlimited. Fillings have ranged from natural to manufactured synthetics. Mattress casings (or ticking) have held straw, hay, wood shavings, jute, silk floss, coconut fibers, wool, cotton linters, feathers, animal hair, cornhusks, grass, recycled fabrics, polyurethane foam, steel springs, water, and air.

One popular and inexpensive stuffing was called "new shoddy," which was the remnants of cloth

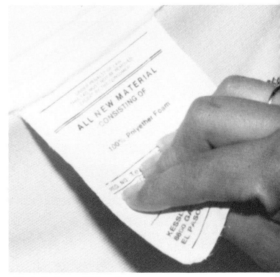

*Photo by Larry Molmud*

*The materials used for the contents of mattresses and box springs have been closely regulated since the Mattress Inspection Act was passed in 1915, pioneering the future course of health and safety standards in the California furniture industry. Courtesy, Western Furnishings Manufacturers Association*

salvaged from the cutting tables in garment factories. It went through "picking machines" to separate the fibers and restore them to the state they were in before being woven into cloth.

There was also an even cheaper stuffing, "secondhand shoddy," made from worn clothing, carpets, and fabric scraps, which were collected by junk and rag peddlers, who put them into bales for sale to manufacturers. Another source of stuffing called "sweepings," consisted of the scraps from mattress covers and upholstered furniture fabrics that fell to the floor; the scraps were then swept up and saved until there was enough to use as stuffing.

Shoddy and sweepings were the subject of a warning memo to the public

issued in 1929 by J.S. Casey, chief of the Division of Weights and Measures, California Department of Agriculture.

*Do not accept or consider a mattress made from shoddy or mill sweepings. The latter is oily and dirty and contains germs picked up through contact with the floor and under the machines. Shoddy is made from old rags or clippings from tailor shops, garment factories and sweat shops. It is cut into small pieces and fed through a machine which tears the cloth apart and shreds [it]. For the sake of your health, it is wise not to use these materials.*

Nevertheless, these recycled products were widely used in the industry for many years, resulting in the coining of the word "shoddy" to mean anything inferior made to seem superior, a development that undoubtedly helped to push along the demand for regulations.

A mattress filled with shoddy or low-grade cotton sold for $3.50 at wholesale and around $6.50 at retail in the early 1900s and usually weighed between 30 and 50 pounds so housewives could flip it.

The manufacture of a mattress was an uncomplicated process. First the cover was sewn on all sides, with a four- to six-inch opening left at one end of the mattress. Next, the picking machine spout blew the stuffing into the opening. The opening's flap was then sewn shut, and employees equipped with paddles would beat the mattress until the filling was evenly distributed throughout. Finally, the bedding was tufted to hold the stuffing in place and a decorative fabric roll was attached around the edges.

The principal problem with all of these stuffings was that no matter what they were called, they were secondhand materials often passed off as new. Frequently, they were dirty, verminous, and potential sources of disease. Clearly something needed to be done.

*Before the introduction of laws governing the furniture industry in the early 1900s, much of the material used for the stuffing of mattresses and other upholstered pieces consisted of "shoddy" and "sweepings." Sources of shoddy ranged from cloth remnants salvaged from garment factories to carpet and fabric scraps collected by junk peddlers, while sweepings were comprised of scraps from mattress covers and upholstery fabrics that were swept up off the floor for future use. These products posed a potential health hazard for the public and became an issue that was soon addressed by the advent of industry standards and regulations. Courtesy, Western Furnishings Manufacturers Association*

*Strict health regulations apply to uphol-*
*stery, quilting, pads, and cushions as well as*
*mattresses thanks to the pioneering efforts*
*of John P. Cleese, a leading San Francisco*
*bedding manufacturer whose work led to the*
*legislation of the Mattress Inspection Act of*
*1915. Courtesy, Western Furnishings*
*Manufacturers Association*

California took the lead in 1909, when alarmed by potential health hazards, the state legislature passed a law requiring that bedding and upholstered furniture, stuffed with secondhand materials, bear a label or stamp "showing the correct character" of the substances. Failure to obey it was a misdemeanor and punishable by a fine, or imprisonment, or both. The new statute was signed into law by Governor James N. Gillette on March 11.

Although it was the first legislation of its kind in the United States, unfortunately it had two major flaws. One was that the law was based on the premise that all the consumer needed was to know what type of stuffing was used. The other flaw was a failure to assign enforcement of the law to a specific state department and give that department the authority and means to enforce it. About the only recourse citizens with a complaint had was to try to interest a public prosecutor in their case, who was usually a busy, overworked civil servant not likely to have much interest in consumer product fraud.

Certainly the law was significant, however poorly drawn, since for the

*Trained craftsmen skillfully construct fine armchairs in this 1950s photo. Note the conveyor belt in the foreground, used to conveniently transport parts throughout the factory. Courtesy, Western Furnishings Manufacturers Association*

first time anywhere it required disclosure of the hidden contents of bedding and upholstered furniture. No one doubted that it was a great step forward for the public and, indeed, for the reputable, honest manufacturer. But lack of attention by succeeding legislatures to the kinds of problems that came from applying it to the industry would cause it to be amended 27 times between 1911 and 1988.

The first amendment was made in 1911 when the legislature added a section that gave the commissioner of the Bureau of Labor Statistics and his deputies "all the powers and authority of sheriffs to make arrests for violation of the provisions of this act."

Finally an agency had been officially assigned to enforce the law. Apparently that was as far as it went; there is no record of the amendment having any affect whatsoever on the industry until John P. Cleese, a prominent San Francisco bedding manufacturer, who had lost a substantial order to an unscrupulous producer not long before, decided to lobby in Sacramento for a law that would work.

The story of Cleese's important role is extracted from a historical monograph printed in the January 1, 1948, Bulletin No. 5, of the Bureau of Furniture and Bedding Inspection.

Cleese first became aware of trouble in the bedding and furniture industry in 1909 when he found that a mattress factory, which had begun after the San Francisco earthquake in 1906, was underselling established factories now that the disaster-created demand had slackened.

To his horror, he discovered that the plant was getting its stuffing materials from old mattresses discarded at the public dump and was labeling them as new. Obviously, they could afford to undercut the competition. Cleese tried to alert dealers to the situation, but was unable to raise much interest. After all, no official was actually checking the tags as required by the new law.

It would take a personal business experience to propel Cleese into full action. His story dramatically illustrates the kind of problem faced by the industry. One of his best customers was a large furniture dealer selling primarily to hotels and apartment buildings. The dealer had informed Cleese that his estimate for furnishing a 200-room hotel had been rejected because of a much lower bid by another store. That meant, of course, Cleese would not get an order either.

Thinking that perhaps the dealer's competitor was using a lower price as a loss leader to get a foot in the door, Cleese decided to investigate. He went

*The Lee-Gingery store on Colorado Street in Glendale featured Stockwell Never Stretch Mattresses and "service that satisfies" in 1932. Courtesy, Security Pacific National Bank Photographic Collection/Los Angeles Public Library*

to the competitor's store, but had to wait while the owner took care of a customer.

Wending his way to the balcony where the office was located, he suddenly heard the owner's voice, loud and clear, floating up from below. He was placing a telephone order with a factory for 200 pure silk floss (kapok) mattresses. The customer, a woman, who had questioned how such quality could be offered at the low price, was satisfied by the call. She confirmed her order and departed, confident she was getting a good deal on quality mattresses.

Cleese, however, noticed that the dealer had not yet hung up the telephone, and the second his customer was out of earshot had spoken into the receiver, asking "Are you still there?" He told the manufacturer to go ahead with the order, but to make the mattresses "fifty percent kapok and fifty percent cotton and put on pure silk floss tags. I'll confirm the order by mail."

Shocked by what he had overheard, Cleese quickly left the store. On the following day, he returned to his own customer to report what he had discovered. He heard someone talking to the owner in the office and waited

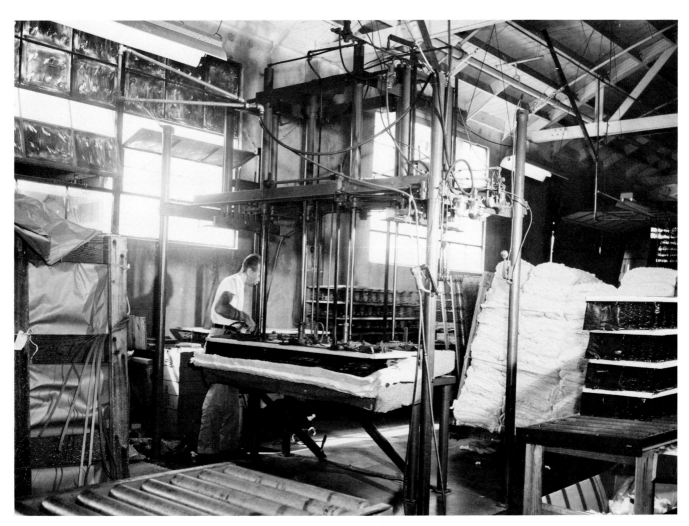

until they were finished. To his surprise, the customer who walked out was the same woman he had seen the previous day in the other store. "If you are $2.50 higher on the mattresses," she was saying, "I think you must be high on all the other stuff, so just forget the hotel."

The mystery of the undercut hotel-bed bid had been solved and Cleese was ready to do battle.

A thoughtful and cautious man, he first wrote to every secretary of state in the country inquiring if they had any law on their books that regulated the manufacture or labeling of mattresses. Each of them replied that they not only didn't have such a law, but had never even heard of one. Cleese then sat down and wrote a list of all the abuses in the mattress business he knew about and outlined the kind of law he felt was needed "to bring all factories up to an honest standard."

He set off for Sacramento for a convention of the California Employers Federation, which he had headed for two terms. Through old friends and fortuitous circumstances, he got help in drafting a bill. It was referred to the Committee on Health and Quarantine because it carried a sterilization provision, and, subsequently, was carried to the assembly and the senate. (In

*The efforts of John P. Cleese resulted in the labeling of all mattresses and upholstered pieces, informing both consumers and industry manufacturers about the true nature of the materials used in each finished product. This benchmark legislation has led to many other sound regulations and restrictions, including California's recent flammability law. A California furniture worker is shown here installing the filling and springs of a sofa. Courtesy, Western Furnishings Manufacturers Association*

*Postwar furniture manufacturers adhered to the strict criteria established for the labeling and grading of their upholstered products. Courtesy, Western Furnishings Manufacturers Association*

his monograph he writes that all this happened in 1911, but no new bedding laws were passed until 1915.)

Cleese recalled that when he stood nervously before the Health and Quarantine Committee, he was convinced he was in a room full of enemies. After he had explained the proposed bill in great detail, he concluded by saying: "There is nothing in this bill to injure any honest manufacturer, and if anyone opposes the bill, they stand for crooked business."

His statement was greeted by clapping and laughter and he wondered what was going on. Committee Chairman Frank Merriam (later governor)

*asked if anyone else was in favor of the bill—no one said anything—so after a few minutes Merriam said, "Is anyone here opposed to the bill?" . . . Senator Scott of San Francisco, a member of the committee, started to laugh and Merriam said, "What are you laughing at?" Scott said, "That is funny—didn't you hear Cleese say that anyone who opposed the bill stood for crooked business, and do you expect anyone to admit he is crooked?" He then made a motion to pass it.*

At first Cleese had wanted to have the use of secondhand materials banned entirely, but eventually settled for basing the bill on labeling that would

show the true contents of the mattress. It was a beginning, more significant, perhaps, than even he realized.

Once the legislature had passed what was known as the Mattress Inspec-tion Act, it was sent to Governor Hiram Johnson for his signature or veto. Cleese arranged to meet Johnson and describes the occasion as follows:

*It was quite warm, the Governor sat at his desk, coat and vest off, his sleeves rolled up and smoking a pipe. After the introduction, he told me to fire away. I took the bill, chapter by chapter, and explained everything to him. When I had finished, he said, "Is there any other state with such a law?" and I told him no. Then he said, "Then we are the pioneers in this law."*

Something else pleased the governor. According to Cleese, the governor added that "This law is something new to us here—we have a business asking the Senate to pass a law to make themselves honest. Generally business fights the Senate interfering in business. If you want, I'll sign it," which he promptly did.

An examination of the 1915 Mattress Inspection Act reveals that it covered a lot more than the simple labeling of mattress filling content, it also included labeling quilted pads, comforters, mattress pads, bunk quilts, cushions stuffed or filled with wool, and hair or other soft material "to be

# Stockwell—My Beauty-Sleep Ensemble

### Construction Details

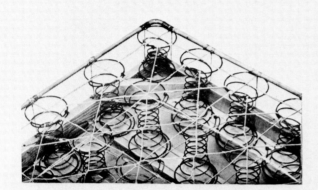

#### STOCKWELL BOX SPRING

### Sturdy · Resilient · Quiet

*The picture above shows the inside construction of the Stockwell Box Spring before application of pad and cover.*

**1** The sturdy braced frame is made of selected kiln dried lumber, lock jointed and glued together—patented features allowing greatly improved construction.

**2** The deep springs with wide centers are of oil tempered steel thus assuring lasting resiliency.

**3** For perfect quiet the springs are mounted on hemp insulation.

**4** Each spring is hand tied 8 times with the finest Italian hemp. Scientific tying results in unusual buoyancy.

**5** The springs are securely bound together along the four edges with rattan. The corners are secured with patented corner irons.

**6** A patented separable pad covers the springs and can be easily taken off.

**7** The outside cover of Stockwell NeverStretch ticking is fastened on with glove clasps and is easily removable for cleaning.

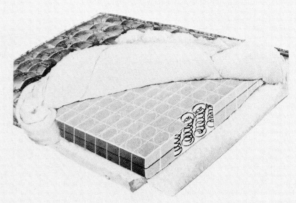

#### STOCKWELL INNER-SPRING MATTRESS

### Assures Correct Sleeping Posture

*The above picture shows the inside construction of this sleep-inviting mattress.*

**1** The cone springs cannot tip, sag or lump. They are woven into a single unit thus giving a mattress of unusual resiliency and assuring correct sleeping posture.

**2** The springs are anchored between double layers of heavy fabric.

**3** The ends of the springs are looped to prevent puncture of ticking.

**4** The spring unit is upholstered with many layers of soft, downy staple cotton and felted linters.

**5** The covering is the famous Stockwell NeverStretch Ticking which cannot stretch or spread.

**6** The mattress is finished with a roll edge thus adding to its appearance and serviceability.

### STOCKWELL-KLING CORPORATION, Los Angeles

---

*The first innerspring mattress was patented in 1900 by James Marshall, signaling the end of the stuffed mattress era. This Stockwell-Kling sleep ensemble boasted sturdy construction, lasting resiliency, and the assurance of a correct sleeping posture. Courtesy, Western Furnishings Manufacturers Association*

used on a couch or other bed for sleeping or reclining purposes."

The tagging requirement was retained in the amended act, but mandated more information. The tag had to state, "in the English language," whether the filling material was new, old, secondhand, or shoddy, and had to include the name of the manufacturer. When more than one new material was used, it also had to give the percentage of each.

Wholesalers and retailers were not forgotten either; they were specifically forbidden from selling untagged or unlabeled merchandise, effectively cutting off that escape route for unprincipled manufacturers. No one was permitted to recycle materials from mattresses used in hospitals, or other institutions treating people with diseases or from shoddy or other used materials, unless they were thoroughly sterilized and disinfected by a process "approved by the Board of Health of the city where said mattress is made, remade or renovated." In 1929 that responsibility was assumed by the state Department of Public Health.

*Carding mattresses was dusty and potentially dangerous work at the Bailey-Schmitz facility in the early days of the mattress and upholstery industry. Courtesy, Security Pacific National Bank Photographic Collection/Los Angeles Public Library*

California's decision to permit the use of sterilized secondhand materials avoided the problems encountered by Pennsylvania and Illinois. A Pennsylvania 1913 bill banned outright the use of shoddy, whether it was sterilized or not, in the manufacture of "comfortables" (stuffed or quilted covers), and inevitably it led to an appeal to the U.S. Supreme Court, which in 1926 declared the law unconstitutional. Illinois passed a similar law in 1915, which was challenged by a Chicago dealer in new and second-hand furniture, who had been fined $25 for not having an information tag on a used felt-filled mattress. The Illinois Supreme Court found the law unconstitutional because it banned the use of materials that could be made safe by "a reasonable regulation," namely, sterilization.

Interestingly, it was California's law that prohibited the detachment of tags for the first time, stating that any "mark or statement placed upon any mattress under the provisions of this act . . ." cannot be removed by any person. Probably two-thirds of California's mattress, pillow, and cushion

*The Furniture Manufacturers Association of Southern California took a prominent role in 1955 in an effort to help increase and refine the regulations governing bedding and upholstery manufacturing. The association proposed a bill that would create an advisory board to oversee the industry. Approved by Governor Goodwin J. Knight on July 5, 1955, this new bill established the advisory board whose initial membership included two manufacturers, two retailers, one supply dealer, and one sterilizer. Courtesy, Western Furnishings Manufacturers Association*

tag-snipping owners could have been charged and found guilty if it had been taken seriously. But its primary intent, in all fairness, was to protect the public from unscrupulous manufacturers and retailers, and eventually it would be amended to reflect that purpose.

How well the regulations were working in California at a time when only two other states, Illinois and Pennsylvania, had any similar laws, can be seen in a report by the Better Business Bureau in 1927. It revealed that the Better Business Bureau, which had established a program called "Bedding and Furniture Service," had hired an investigator to look into the problem of mislabeling furniture and bedding by manufacturers and retailers. The report concluded, "Under his direction, this condition has been corrected to the point where it is now a rule instead of an exception for bedding and furniture to be correctly labeled."

Over the years, the overall statute would be amended, expanded, strengthened, and changed, particularly since manufacturing technology itself changed.

For example, when the first innerspring mattress with steel coils and individual cloth pockets was patented in 1900 by James Marshall, a 60-year-old Canadian planing mill operator, the future of fully stuffed mattresses began to dim, and new regulations would reflect that development. For a while, Marshall produced the coils for the ventilated mattresses in a one-room shop, but the new product didn't really get going until John Gail of the Simmons Company invented a machine to do it all mechanically.

Eventually the innerspring mattress became enormously popular. In 1925 Simmons' "Beautyrest" sold for $39.50, several times the price of the best solid pad mattress, and it would not be long before most of the traditional fillings would be abandoned and fully stuffed mattresses largely relegated to the secondhand market.

In 1927 the California legislature decided that the state government should stop financing the cost of enforcing the labeling law (still under the Bureau of Labor Statistics), and made it mandatory for manufacturers, sterilizers, and vendors of bedding and upholstered furniture to obtain licenses by paying fees to the Department of Agriculture.

In 1929 the Division of Weights and Measures replaced the Bureau of Labor Statistics as the specific department responsible for implementing the new mattress law and was given powers to handle the licensing, administration, and enforcement. It was also instructed to adopt standards for labeling and grading materials; to enter businesses where mattresses were manufactured, sterilized, or sold; to examine records, and condemn or seize products in violation of the act. The state Department of Public Health got an even more drastic power: Destroy any mattress found to be unsanitary.

The proliferation of manufacturers, distributors, and sterilizers, along with the growth in California's population, moved the state legislature to create a separate Bureau of Furniture and Bedding Inspection in 1935, inserting it into the Department of Professional and Vocational Standards. Despite that centralization, the separate statutes for bedding and upholstered furniture remained intact until 1939 when the Furniture and Bedding Inspection Act brought them both under a single statute, which by now had clout.

The legislation specifically named mislabeling, false advertising, and misrepresentation (even though they were already covered in California's general law) as punishable crimes. It was the legislature's direct response to the problem of misleading advertisements and other cons being used to promote

*Facing page: Recognized for their work on behalf of the Industrial Relations Council of Furniture Manufacturers of Southern California, Henry Brandler (left foreground) and Joseph Siskin (right foreground) were honored in November 1958 with a breakfast celebration and a gift of luggage in show of appreciation for their services. Cited for their success in negotiating contracts with the furniture industry unions, Brandler, executive vice president of the L.A. Period Furniture Manufacturing Company and Siskin, president of the Angelus Furniture Manufacturing Company, posed with other industry leaders to document this notable event. Courtesy, Western Furnishings Manufacturers Association*

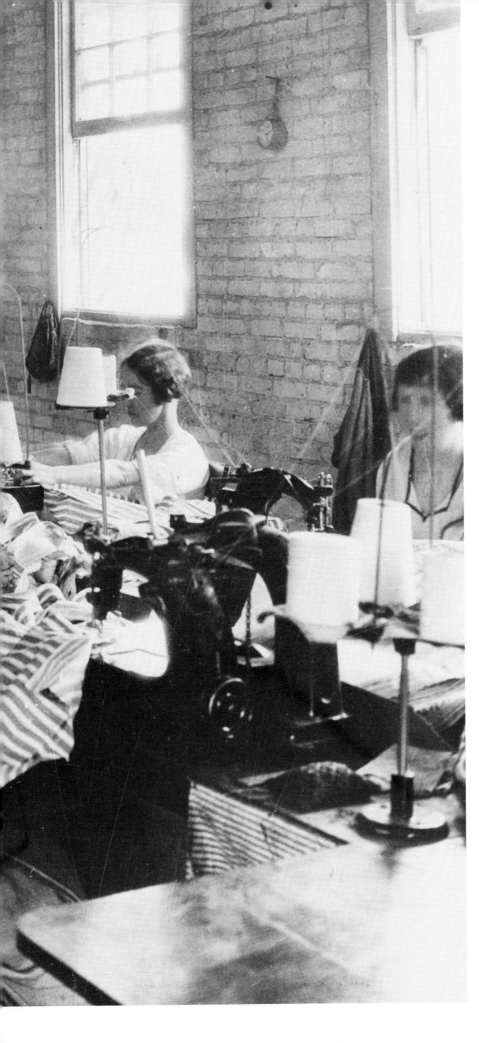

*These women busily sewed ticking for the mattresses manufactured at the Bailey-Schmitz company under the watchful eye of their supervisor in the 1930s. Courtesy, Security Pacific National Bank Photographic Collection/Los Angeles Public Library*

*While legislation was being passed regarding the health and safety regulations of furniture and bedding, special care was also being introduced into the manufacturing workplace in the 1960s. In an effort to reduce the worker's exposure to finishing materials, spray booths used a special air cleaning system to maintain a balanced vapor-free atmosphere. Finishing materials were stored in separate concrete vaults and were piped to each work station. Courtesy, Western Furnishings Manufacturers Association*

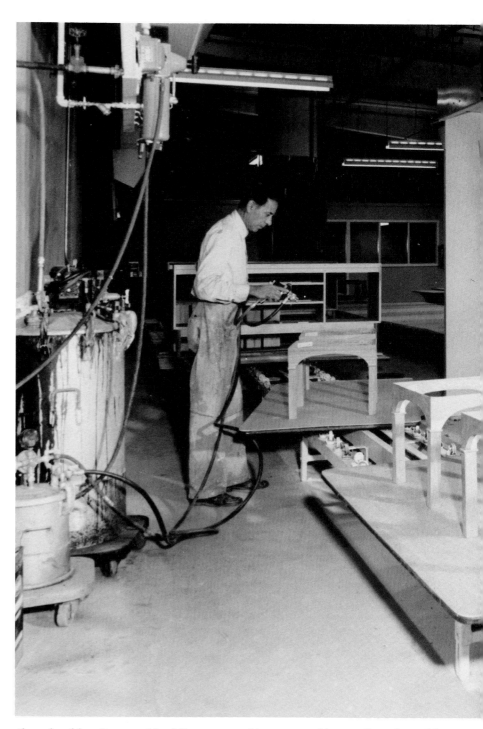

the sale of furniture and bedding, some of it promoted by retailers the public regarded as trustworthy.

The advertisements would offer items at a price deeply discounted from a much higher figure, which, in fact, had never existed. A similar ploy featured big, banner-like ribbons on mattresses showing the supposed retail price. Although those figures also were fictitious, the dealer would offer to sell the mattress at a significantly reduced price. Another scam was used to sell products like pillows by putting a manufacturer's label on them that showed, for

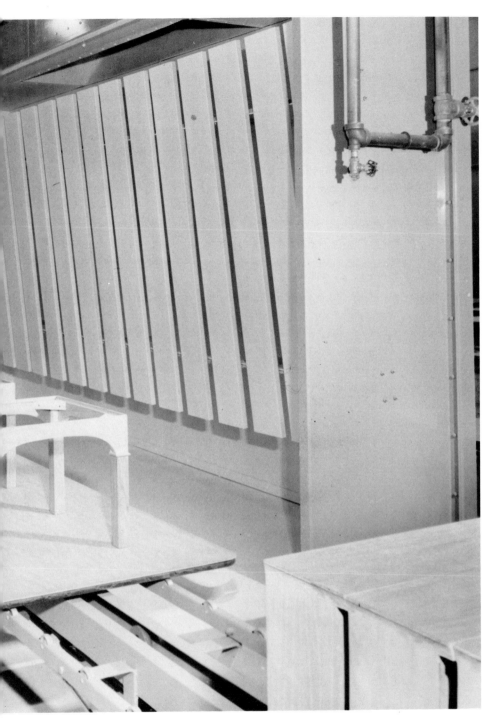

example, that they were filled completely with expensive down. In truth, they were only 80 percent down and 20 percent feathers—a small falsehood perhaps, but one that added up to a lot of dollars.

The 1939 revision of the law also included a change that permitted Hollywood movie companies to sell upholstered furniture and bedding used for sets in their films, as new, if they had been made from all new materials. Because set designers bought substantial quantities of furniture, this was an attractive plus, but it was fated to have a short life and was repealed in 1941,

*Facing page: Air-driven staplers were in-vented in 1948 offering many time-saving benefits without any loss of quality, thus re-placing the need for skilled upholsterers or "tack spitters" upon whom the furniture industry once relied. Courtesy, Senco Products, Inc.*

returning the practice to the secondhand category.

In that same year, extensive revisions in the regulations on furniture and bedding were made, bringing to light so many shortcomings, oversights, and omissions that a mammoth 10 pages of amendments were signed into law by Governor Culbert L. Olsen. But that was nothing compared with what happened 10 years later, when 90 sections of the law were added, deleted, or amended.

Strangely, the Furniture Manufacturers Association assumed a passive sideline role during all of the political activities and maneuvering that went on over the years in the areas of upholstered furniture and bedding. It wasn't until 1955, when the Furniture Manufacturers Association of Southern California (FMASC) took the kind of leadership role that the industry sorely needed. (The FMASC was the successor to the FMA and the predecessor of today's WFMA.)

The FMASC set in motion landmark legislation that would put the furniture and bedding industry on a par with other regulated businesses and professions in California that already were overseen by boards or commissions composed of their own representatives. A bill was drafted that would create a similar organization for the furniture industry to which the chief of the Bureau of Furniture and Bedding Inspection would be responsive. The bill was given to Assemblyman Frank Bonelli to carry into the legislature.

Some members of the legislature felt adding any more regulatory boards to those already in existence was a bad idea; the bill was modified to create an advisory board instead. Its membership would consist of two manufacturers, two retailers, one supply dealer, and one sterilizer. Later, in 1961, the requirements would be changed to include one manufacturer and one retailer to eliminate the possibility of two upholstery or two bedding manufacturers serving simultaneously.

The FMASC, however, noted that the public was becoming increasingly critical and suspicious of businesses and professions that were regulated solely by their own members. So in an innovative move that the legislature would eventually replicate for all boards and commissions, the association added a public member to the industry's advisory board.

The bill sailed through the assembly and the senate and, on July 5, 1955, it was approved by Governor Goodwin J. Knight.

Although its function was designated as advisory, the new board had some real authority. It could refuse to issue a license to any individuals or corporations it had previously disciplined. In a way, it was a case of the good guys

finally winning out over the bad guys in an industry that for too long had not had very much control of its own household.

In 1959 another significant statutory change occurred when the chief of Furniture and Bedding Inspection became an appointment of the governor to "serve at his pleasure," making the post a political selection. The chief, however, continued to be responsible to the director of what was then called Professional and Vocational Standards; today this organization is known as the Department of Consumer Affairs.

Water beds, which first undulated into life in California, got their share of attention from the legislature. Called "flotation bedding" by the industry, they were added to the list of filling materials as "liquid" in 1971. The Bureau of Furniture and Bedding Inspection was instructed to come up with regulations that would cover the quality of their construction as well as their effect on the safety and health of the people who used them. Earlier, legislation had been passed forbidding landlords to turn away tenants who owned water beds, so long as appropriate insurance was carried. Landlords were worried about the possible damage that could be caused to their property by weight and water leaks.

Flammability eventually replaced inferior stuffing as the top public concern among the bedding and upholstered furniture industry. The California legislature ruled in 1970 that all mattresses made in the state must use flame-retardant material. Initially, upholstered furniture was not included in the decree, but it was added in 1972. Reupholstered furniture containing fillings joined the list in 1984.

Then in 1974 the legislature dropped a national blockbuster. Starting in

1975, all upholstered furniture imported from outside the state had to meet California's stringent fire-retardant standards. Predictably, when confronted by the costly prospect of having to produce each piece to two different standards, one for the California market and one for the rest of the country, out-of-state manufacturers went into orbit, or to be more precise, into court through an organization called the Upholstered Furniture Action Council (UFAC).

The battle became a lot like a tug-of-war contest, first one side gaining and then the other, with no apparent winner identifiable. UFAC pulled its California opponents almost over the line when it got an injunction to prevent enforcement of the new law by the Bureau of Furniture and Bedding Inspection. The injunction held while the federal district court examined whether the federal Flammability Fabrics Act and the Consumer Products Safety Act preempted California's right to regulate upholstered furniture safety within its borders. Then it was California's turn to tug when U.S. District Judge Philip C. Wilkins dismissed the complaint.

UFAC promptly asked the California Furniture Manufacturers Association to intervene on UFAC's behalf and requested that a three-judge court consider the constitutional issues involved. But the court sent the problem, apparently unresolved, back to Judge Wilkins. He then changed the original decision, saying that it was incorrect. His rationale was that Congress did intend the Flammable Fabrics Act to establish uniform standards throughout the country, and California's tougher law would thwart that intention. Consequently, he ordered an injunction against the California Bureau of Home Furnishings.

But that didn't last long either and was dissolved by the court. So the UFAC went back to the three-judge court in a case known as *Upholstered Furniture Action Council v. California Bureau of Home Furnishings*. For those readers still able to follow this somewhat bewildering series of events, the outcome was a ruling that California's flammability law was not a violation of the commerce clause of the U.S. Constitution. Therefore, national upholstered furniture manufacturers who wanted to do business would have to comply with it or stay out of the state. Most opted to comply, rather than lose the lucrative California market.

Today, 33 states have followed suit to one degree or another with their own laws regulating the manufacture and sale of bedding and upholstered furniture. But it should come as no surprise that the lead, as so often has been the case in the American furniture industry, had come from the state that enlivened the design world with the California Look.

# A Look at the Future
## by Les Riddell
### Executive Vice President
### of the Western Furnishings Manufacturers Association

One of the rewarding things about looking back at the past from the perspective of the present, as the author has done in this book, is that it provides a base to take an informed peek into the future.

Like all industries, furniture has and always will have, cyclical ups and downs that astute market players take in stride, but never for granted. Wars and the threat of wars, the white-knuckle uncertainties of economic cliffhangers, shifts in social values and directions, demographic changes, and a myriad of expected and unexpected fluctuations affect all who are in business.

But some are luckier than others because the products of their industries are essential to people's lives. True, choices are exercised by their customers in terms of quality, design, color, materials, and, of course, price, but in the end everyone needs some kind of home furnishings, whatever manufacturer they select or retail firm they buy from.

It is that individual competition for market that keeps the furniture business healthy, while our strength comes from standing together as an industry with our collective eyes fixed on the good and the bad happening within and without.

In the 1990s, we are focused on the good that is here and also the good that lies ahead.

Leading manufacturers see the last decade of the twentieth century as a period of continued growth for the California furniture industry. Consumer spending on home furnishings and fixtures will go on rising faster than disposable personal income as the formation of new families increases and the aging of the baby boom population adds its own impetus to the market. And, with no end in sight to the constantly escalating prices of homes, more and more people will expand and fix up their existing houses rather than buy new ones. That development, when coupled with the wide availability of tax-deductible home-equity loans for household furnishings and other improvements, will also enhance the market demand.

Other positive factors will include the industry's response to competition from both furniture imports and other durable goods by consolidating at the manufacturing level to achieve greater economies in purchasing, production, and marketing. In concert with that strategy, the coming years will also bring the emergence of large holding companies with several name-brand lines that will include home, office, and other commercial and institutional furnishings and accessories.

During the late 1980s, a significant turnaround in the export of furniture began to develop and is expected to continue. Foreign buyers have become much more willing to look at American products because of prices that are attractive, relative to those of European and Japanese exports. That has come about as the direct result of the response by U.S. furniture manufacturers to the rapid acceleration of imports that began in the 1980s. Realizing the need for greater marketing clout, they introduced advanced technology to lower manufacturing costs, making their products more competitive.

Paralleling those efforts to counter imports and strengthen sales, the industry also successfully lobbied for federal trade legislation that has placed import restrictions on those countries that engage in unfair trade practices.

In another important area, the industry will respond to the ever-increasing fast pace of American business by introducing quicker delivery service and by shipping a wider variety of product than ever before.

All of these advances are tempered somewhat by California's high costs of doing business, its expensive land and housing, and tightly regulated commercial climate, which will continue to force some manufacturers to seek out-of-state facilities.

However, on the other side of the coin, the potential in the Golden State is enormous. Quantifying the vast California market is almost like describing a separate country. Virtually a "nation," with some 28 million people who have an effective buying income exceeding $426 billion, it ranks first among the 50 states in population, purchasing power, retail sales, and a host of other market indicators.

On a global scale, California has one of the largest economies in the world, producing more cotton than Egypt and more computers than Japan. If it were a separate country, its per capita GNP would rank sixth, surpassing the U.S. itself, West Germany, and virtually every other industrialized nation.

Operating within that mind-boggling kind of market, California furniture manufacturing firms, their suppliers and retail outlets can look to a future filled with unlimited opportunities for unprecedented prosperity. Granted the challenges are many, but the industry's inherent stability and vigor will take it into the twenty-first century stronger than at any time in its long and illustrious history.

# CHAPTER SIX

# Partners In Progress

Almost since the birth of this nation more than two centuries ago, the southeastern region has been widely recognized as the furniture-manufacturing hub of the United States. But the move westward has had its impact on that industry, and today California ranks second in the nation in furniture production.

Much of it is centered in the five-county Southern California region, where nearly 1,200 furniture manufacturers are headquartered. Statewide the industry employs some 58,000 workers, more than two-thirds of them in Los Angeles County alone. Estimates by the American Furniture Manufacturers Association indicate that more than 10 percent of home-furniture production (about $1.5 billion) is done in California.

The growth of the industry in the state is not surprising, as California is by far the largest furniture marketplace in the nation, accounting for about 12 percent of sales. In addition to the state's population explosion, freight costs have risen sharply, curtailing the ability of East Coast firms to compete in the western region.

The following pages tell the stories of a few of the companies that have helped make California such an important furniture-manufacturing center. They represent a broad cross section of the industry, some producing finished goods, others producing components and accessories, and others the tools to assemble them. There are small companies, with as few as 15 employees, and large ones, with 10,000 or more in their work force.

There are new businesses and old ones. The newest was launched in 1986; the oldest has been in business for more than 125 years. Most of these companies were started in Southern California and are still run by the founders and/or their descendants. Others are publicly owned; one is listed on the New York Stock Exchange, another on the American Stock Exchange.

There is a strong entrepreneurial flavor in these stories. In typical fashion, several were started in home garages, others in backyards, bedrooms, or apartment studios. One was launched by a Russian immigrant who spoke no English, another by a former U.S. government agent who developed the concept for his product while traveling on riverboats in the jungles of Ecuador.

Collectively, these companies produce virtually every conceivable line of furniture in nearly every price range. Some of it is packed in cartons, ready to be taken home and assembled. Some is custom designed and produced to order. There is furniture for every room in the house and for commercial, industrial, and institutional use. As befits the California life-style, there are hammocks and patio furniture as well. Some of the companies represented here produce furniture components, including hardware, glass, felt, fabric, and foam.

Not all are exclusively California companies. One is headquartered in Japan and others in the eastern and midwestern United States. They have all, however, played an important part in the growth of the California furniture industry and have chosen to give their patronage and support to this important literary and civic project.

*In the 1950s the awards banquet of the Furniture Manufacturers Association of Southern California featured honored guest General Omar Nelson Bradley (center), pictured here with leading industry figures (from left to right), Richard Sax, Jack Mallerstein, Joseph Siskin, and Eddy Feldman. The swank El Mirador in Palm Springs hosted this gala event. Courtesy, Western Furnishings Manufacturers Association*

# WESTERN FURNISHINGS MANUFACTURERS ASSOCIATION

The Western Furnishings Manufacturers Association (WFMA), formerly the California Furniture Manufacturers Association, traces its origins to Los Angeles in 1911, when a group of Southern California manufacturers decided a trade association would be in their mutual interests.

The name Furniture Manufacturers Association (FMA) was eventually chosen, and dues were set at five dollars per quarter. A mere 12 companies were represented at that initial meeting. None is any longer in business but the association they launched is still going strong.

At the start, FMA had no office space, and its meetings were rotated among the factories of the member companies. The primary areas of concern for the association included labor, credit, delivery, and "general cooperation." The most volatile issue of the day involved the open showroom policy of some manufacturers, who allowed so-called "furniture dealers" with no retail outlets of their own to bring their customers directly to the factory, thus bypassing the furniture retailer. Despite strong, ongoing opposition from the Retail Furniture Association, it was not until 1928 that a resolution was adopted by FMA

*Past and present WFMA presidents celebrate another successful year (from left): Al Sandberg, 1990 president; Gene Rothstein, 1976 president; Jerry Guyre, 1988 president; Burt Grimes, 1990 president-elect; and Richard Mills, 1989 president.*

prohibiting its members from operating open showrooms.

The association moved into its own Los Angeles offices in 1920 and remained in that city until April 1988, when it opened its present headquarters at 12631 East Imperial Highway in Santa Fe Springs. Although the organization has maintained its separate identity continuously since 1911, it has undergone several name changes. In 1949 it became the Furniture Manufacturers Association of Southern California, and later the word "Southern" was dropped. Then it became the California Furniture Manufacturers Association, retaining that name until November 20, 1989, when it became WFMA.

Heading the organization today is executive vice-president Les Riddell, who joined CFMA in 1985, succeeding the retired Lee Hahn, who had served in that capacity for 20 years. Prior to Hahn, Eddy G. Feldman had held the post for many years, beginning in 1945. More than 40 years later he continues to serve the organization as its general counsel.

Affiliated with WFMA and a co-sponsor of this book is the Association of Western Furniture Suppliers (AWFS). A former chapter of WFMA, it became an independent organization in 1979, although the two groups retain close ties, sharing **office space and staff. In addition to**

*Association president Jerry Guyre (right) presents the 1988 Manufacturer of the Year Award to Paul Martinez of Fair Line Furniture Mfg.*

his WFMA duties, Riddell is also executive director of AWFS.

Today the primary activities of WFMA include full-service credit reporting and insurance programs, educational seminars and workshops, and an extensive traffic program. WFMA also retains a lobbyist in Sacramento. Once a year, in cooperation with nine other associations, it hosts a national all-industry convention.

WFMA also maintains close ties with the American Furniture Manufacturers Association (AFMA), headquartered in High Point, North Carolina, and its members enjoy participation in the national body. The latter group also represents WFMA in its lobbying activities in Washington and is accorded the same privileges by WFMA in Sacramento.

The growth of the furniture industry in California and its ranking as the second-largest furniture-producing state and the largest furniture market in the nation is due in large measure to the vision and the efforts of the 150 members of the Western Furnishings Manufacturers Association and the 340 members of the Association of Western Furniture Suppliers.

# ALMAC FELT CO.

*Al Friedman (left) and Jeff Friedman.*

Al K. Friedman, the founder and owner of City of Industry-based Almac Felt Co., has been in the furniture industry in California for 43 years, but got into this particular phase of it more or less by accident. Perhaps "by necessity" would be a more accurate description.

Back in 1965, when a large cotton shipment he needed for his Cadillac Furniture Industries failed to arrive, Friedman decided to stop relying on outside sources for his cotton needs. Going to a sheriff's sale, he purchased his first garnett machine. It was to be the start of a new business.

Friedman is almost a California native, having come here from New York with his family when he was two years old. He graduated from UCLA in 1941 and joined what was then the U.S. Army Air Corps. Five

years and two crashes later, he was discharged and returned to Southern California.

In 1947 Friedman and his brother formed Almac Fixture Company, which manufactured display fixtures. Two years later he purchased a plating shop called Almac Plating and started producing dinette sets under the name of Cadillac Chrome. As he expanded his furniture lines, he changed the name to Cadillac Furniture Industries.

After his initial purchase of a garnett machine, which rips apart raw cotton and re-forms it into rolls and batts, he saw a need for these products and began acquiring additional machines to meet the demand. These are the same type of machines that produce polyester

and carpet padding.

The name of the organization, which had been located at 28th Street and Central Avenue in Los Angeles, was changed to Almac Felt Co. In 1973 it moved into a leased 17,000-square-foot facility in the City of Industry.

The firm's continued growth dictated the need for even larger facilities. Friedman purchased land in Chino and the company moved into a new 55,000-square-foot plant in December 1989. Since 1973 the business has quadrupled and now ships 50,000 pounds of cotton per day. The number of employees has grown from five to more than 35, working in two shifts, and Almac may be the largest producer of cotton felt west of the Mississippi.

Friedman claims the success of his products lies in the "mix." That mix includes boric acid, which is added to the cotton to make it flame-retardant. Principal customers are manufacturers of furniture, mattresses, and futons.

Friedman's son, Steven, is a vice-president of the company but, as a practicing attorney, is not involved in its day-to-day affairs. A second son, Jeffrey, sells filling materials for Almac and other companies.

Al Friedman has been active for many years in the Western Furnishings Manufacturers Association. He has been a member of the board of directors and served as secretary in 1971-1972 and in 1972-1973. He is also the recipient of several awards from the organization. Almac is presently purchasing additional machines and expects to double production within the year.

It was David Christy who, in 1855, wrote "Cotton is King." If so, Al Friedman must certainly be considered a high-ranking member of the royal family.

# MONTEREY FURNITURE

As a boy growing up in Burbank, where he was born, Kei Higashi never even thought of the furniture industry as his life's work. His father was a farmer, and Kei fully expected to follow in his footsteps. Then came the outbreak of World War II, which was to dramatically alter his life.

With thousands of other Japanese-Americans, the Higashi family was shipped off to an Arizona relocation center. Kei was released in order to continue his education and, shortly thereafter, was drafted into the U.S. Army. Following his discharge in 1946, he settled in Glendale. Unsure of his future direction, he still harbored thoughts of agriculture, until a friend who worked for a furniture manufacturing company suggested Kei apply for a job there. He was hired, marking the start of a career that has extended over more than four decades.

The young man was hardworking and ambitious and, after only one year, became a foreman. He remained with the company until 1960, when he moved to another furniture business. Three years later he decided the time had come to strike out on his own, and Monterey Furniture was born.

The business was originally located in a rented 20,000-square-foot facility at 540 Monterey Pass Road in Monterey Park. It was more space than Higashi needed, but it was available at a reasonable rate, and he had faith in his ability to make his new venture grow. Starting with

about six employees, the company grew to 60 within four years, justifying Higashi's faith.

Monterey Furniture specializes in the manufacture of high-quality upholstered living room furniture. Sales are primarily made through decorators and specifiers to residential users. The company still does some commercial business, although it got out of the contract end of the industry in 1975. Monterey has enjoyed steady growth and, in 1988, moved into its present facilities at 5160 Commerce Drive in Baldwin Park, where it occupies 20,000 square feet of leased space. The bulk of the firm's sales are in Southern California, with some in Arizona and Northern California.

In 1972 Monterey

Furniture purchased Alu-Mont Furniture Manufacturing Corp., a manufacturer of aluminum patio furniture headquartered in Monterey Park, where it had been founded in 1966. The opportunity to

*TOP: Guy Higashi is president of the parent company, Monterey Furniture.*

*BOTTOM: Kei Higashi (center), founder and chairman of the board of Monterey Furniture, with sons Guy (left) and Kent (right), who have played major roles in the operation of the family businesses.*

*TOP: Alu-Mont Furniture Manufacturing Corp., purchased in 1972, is under the guidance of president Kent Higashi.*

*BOTTOM: Alu-Mont Furniture Manufacturing Corp. occupies this 110,000-square-foot facility at 5400 Irwindale Avenue, Irwindale.*

acquire it was presented to Higashi by his sales representative, who sold for both companies. Somewhat reluctantly, because of the wide difference in product line, Higashi made a low offer, which the Alu-Mont owners accepted.

Today Alu-Mont has become larger than its parent company. Its lines of patio furniture are produced and sold in mass, compared with the more customized approach of Monterey Furniture. About 75 per-

cent of sales are for home use, with the balance used in commercial applications. Its products are sold in the 11 western states and Hawaii. In 1982 Alu-Mont built its own 110,000-square-foot facility at 5400 Irwindale Avenue in Irwindale. It employs about 60 people during its peak seasons.

Kei Higashi's sons, Guy and Kent, play major roles in the operations of the two companies. Guy is president of Monterey Furniture,

and Kent serves as president of Alu-Mont. Kei is chairman of the board of Monterey Furniture, which was incorporated in 1964 and is the parent company.

The senior Higashi has long been active in industry and community activities. He is currently serving his second term as a member of the board of directors of the Western Furnishings Manufacturers Association. He has lived in Monterey Park for more than 30 years and, in 1974, served as president of that city's chamber of commerce. A former member of Rotary, he has also been active in the Girls and Boys Club of Monterey Park. He is chairman of the Monterey Park Salvation Army Advisory Board and a past president of the Boy Scout Council of the San Gabriel Valley. His office walls are lined with awards from the Boy Scouts and other organizations he has served.

Also adorning his walls are photos, trophies, and other mementos of his far-flung hunting and fishing expeditions. Until recently, he made annual trips that took him to nearly every corner of the world, hunting big game.

Kei Higashi may not have planned on a career in the furniture industry where, according to him, it is rare to find people of Japanese ancestry, for whom agriculture is far more traditional. But he is justifiably proud of the success he has achieved and of the two sons who are carrying on so well in the new Higashi family tradition.

# McFLEM CHAIR MANUFACTURING COMPANY, INC.

It was the young but rapidly growing television industry that gave McFlem Furniture Manufacturing Company its start. The time was the early 1950s, and the proud owner of his first television would find neighbors dropping by every evening to see this latest wonder of technology. Providing seats for everyone to watch Uncle Miltie became a problem—one that Herman McGill, Richard Flemion, and their wives, Edylene and Dee Dee, respectively, decided to solve.

And so in 1951 a new company was formed by each couple contributing $200 in working capital. The fledgling operation began producing small, sturdy upholstered chairs that were ideal for TV viewing. Their stationary chair sold for $9.95 and the rocker for $13.95. Each chair was strong enough to support a truck—a feature used in early advertising campaigns.

The firm began operations in a rented garage next to a home in Downey, but within two months it had moved into a 2,000-square-foot barn in El Segundo. At first, Herman McGill and Richard Flemion kept their daytime jobs at Interstate Engineering, building their chairs at night. They had one full-time employee and a part-time sales representative, plus their wives and two other part-time employees.

Each day, Edylene and Dee Dee would rent a trailer and deliver the chairs that had been completed the previous evening. With no furniture experience and only the barest knowledge of upholstery, the principals learned on the job by trial and error. At first, none of them received any income from the business, and the one full-time employee was paid one dollar an hour.

One of the first sales was to Hub Furniture, which agreed to buy 100 rockers if the price were reduced by

*It can honestly be claimed that a McFlem chair can support the weight of a truck—as cofounder Herman McGill demonstrated in 1953.*

one dollar per chair. The salesman quickly agreed, and, needing a name to put on the purchase order, coined the name McFlem on the spot, using the first syllable of each partner's last name.

In 1956 the company, which had incorporated two years earlier, moved to a 12,000-square-foot location in Hawthorne. At that point Herman and Richard quit their jobs to work full time in their rapidly expanding business. That same year they opened a branch operation in Cleveland, Oklahoma, run by Herman McGill's brother-in-law, Roy R. Rogers, and his wife, Anna May, who was Edylene McGill's sister. The branch was closed a year later, and the Rogerses joined the California company.

The Hawthorne factory into which the firm moved had been occupied by a poker table manufacturer, which left behind inventory, machinery, and supplies. So McFlem temporarily sold poker tables in order to use up the inventory. At the same time, its regular business was expanding to include recliners, followed by lounge chairs, sofas, and, eventually, a full line of upholstered furniture.

In 1957 McGill bought out the Flemions, and the company is now wholly owned by McGill and his two sons, Eddie L. and Michael R. McGill. All three are still active in the company.

McFlem continued its rapid growth, and in 1962 it moved to a second Hawthorne facility. This property consisted of two side-by-side 10,000-square-foot buildings, which were combined by knocking out a wall. One of the buildings had housed a doll manufacturer that had gone out of business, leaving behind thousands of doll parts. As it had with poker tables, McFlem diversified temporarily, using up inventory and making space for its own products. The last of the dolls were donated to the City of El Segundo, which used them for charitable fund-raising purposes.

Herman McGill was very active in El Segundo for many years. A longtime member of the city council, he also served as mayor from 1964 to 1968. His last council term

*Herman McGill prepares to turn the first spadeful of dirt at the ground-breaking ceremony of McFlem's new plant in 1967. Looking on are (from left) Michael, Eddie, and Edylene McGill; Roy and Anna May Rogers; and original employee Ollie Cassity.*

was from 1970 to 1974.

In 1967 the firm purchased property at 200 West 138th Street in Los Angeles County and built its current 55,000-square-foot facility. Forty percent of it is owned by Anna Rogers, while Herman McGill and his two sons each own 20 percent.

From a single-fabric, single-color product, McFlem now produces a broad range of high-quality upholstered furniture available in up to 500 fabrics, each in a variety of colors. The company sells primarily to independent, upscale contemporary retail furniture stores. The number of full-time employees has grown

from one to about 90.

Herman McGill continues as president of the company he co-founded, and his sons serve as vice-presidents. Both started working for their father at an early age. After school and during summer vacations, they would sweep out the plant and perform other routine tasks. After joining the firm on a full-time basis, they gradually took

on more and more responsibility and have worked in every phase of the business. Today they have been joined by a third generation of McGills. Eddie's sons, Patrick and Shawn; his daughter, Kimberly; and Michael's daughter, Crystal, are at middle-management positions in the company.

Today the firm does business primarily as MCF Furniture, although its legal designation is still McFlem Chair Manufacturing Company, Inc.—the spur-of-the-moment name invented by an enterprising representative anxious to make his first big sale. The rest, as they say, is history.

# LEWIS INDUSTRIES

When Bernard Lewis, the late founder of Lewis Industries, was in college, the furniture industry was certainly not in his career plans. Originally enrolled in the early 1940s as a pre-law student at the University of Southern California, he switched to pre-dental studies, hoping to complete his education before entering military service. In 1947, however, he contracted a severe case of mononucleosis, which, while temporary, would mean a permanent change in his life.

Still weak from the aftereffects of the disease, Lewis decided to look for an interim job that would require little if any exertion. A family friend suggested a firm that needed a temporary bookkeeper. It was in the textile and foam latex supply industry, and it launched a career for Bernard Lewis that was to last for 40 years.

Because he had his own car, Lewis was soon asked to try his hand at outside sales, at which he was very successful. He quickly moved to

*RIGHT: Bernard Lewis checks a packing slip in the building at 2009 East 25th Street in 1969.*

*BELOW: Bernard Lewis (right) receives the 1986 Supplier of the Year Award from Wayne Anderson, the 1985 recipient.*

sales manager and then general manager. In 1957 he joined another latex manufacturer as general manager, and remained there for several years.

On March 20, 1968, he formed his own company, Lewis Foam, which soon converted completely from latex to urethane foam. On two occasions, the young operation suffered severe fires, the first in the original location at Fourth and Alameda in Los Angeles, and the second three months later in its temporary facilities. On both occasions the firm was quickly back in business, thanks in great measure to the help Bernard Lewis received from his many friends in the industry. These friendships were largely the result of his lifelong policies of honesty, excellent service, and hard work.

Despite the early setbacks, the company, now Lewis Industries, has grown steadily. The original staff of five, which included Lewis and his

wife, Marilyn, now numbers about 175. In 1969 the firm moved into a 15,000-square-foot plant at 2009 East 25th Street in Los Angeles. Within 10 years it added four 20,000-square-foot properties on the same street, giving it a total of 95,000 square feet.

In November 1984 Lewis Industries moved to its present facilities at 10035 Geary Avenue in Santa Fe Springs, a new 150,000-square-foot plant on land it had purchased. By this time Bernard Lewis was chairman of the board, having sold the company two years earlier to his son-in-law, Al Van Bastelaar, who was president. The two men and Aleta Van Bastelaar, Lewis' daughter, made up the board of directors.

Two more tragedies soon struck, making the earlier fires pale in significance. In January 1985 Marilyn Lewis died of cancer. In July 1987, three months after remarrying, Bernard, along with his bride, Elayne, and the Van Bastelaars were killed in the crash of a plane owned and piloted by the younger man.

venture will be moved to a separate plant within two years.

The officers of Lewis Industries are very active in industry organizations, continuing a tradition begun by Bernard Lewis, whose philosophy was "to give back something of ourselves to the industry that supports our business." Lewis himself was honored in 1985 as Supplier of the Year by the Association of Western Furniture Suppliers. Roger Coffey now serves on the association's board of directors, and Terri McCormick is a past president of its

*Aleta and Al Van Bastelaar stand on the future site of Lewis Industries' Santa Fe Springs plant (left). In November 1984 the company moved into its new, modern facility (below) at 10035 Geary Avenue.*

Despite this sudden and terrible loss, the company survived, a tribute to the solid foundation Bernard Lewis had given it. A new management team was appointed, headed by Roger Coffey, president, who had started with the organization in 1978 as a salesman and was sales manager at the time of the accident. Aiding him are administrative director Terri McCormick, accounting manager Evelyn Sheppard, and plant manager Jose Benavides, all of whom have at least 15 years of service with the firm.

The primary business today is the fabrication of flexible urethane foam, sold to furniture and bedding manufacturers and to packaging companies. Some of the other various end-use applications are van conversions, shoulder pads, and aircraft seating. The bulk of sales are in Southern California, yet the firm has become the largest independent fabricator west of the Mississippi River.

In conjunction with foam fabrication, Lewis Industries has long been

a major manufacturer of sofa-sleeper mattresses sold to the furniture-manufacturing industry. In early 1989 it launched a new division called Restwell Bedding. The firm now manufactures a full line of mattresses under the label of Restonic Corp., a nationally recognized mattress manufacturer. Currently operating from the same facility as Lewis, the new

Young Furniture Associates division.

As it enters the last decade of the twentieth century, Lewis Industries continues to be the strong, solid company founded and fashioned by Bernard Lewis—pioneer, innovator, risk-taker, but a strong believer in the old-fashioned virtues of hard work, honesty, and quality.

# LEGGETT & PLATT

J.P. Leggett and C.B. Platt, founders of Leggett & Platt, were residents of Carthage, a county seat in southwest Missouri, when they formed their business partnership in 1883. Leggett was the inventor, having several diverse patents to his credit. When he developed an idea for a coil bedspring, he went to Platt, who was his brother-in-law, for manufacturing capability and expertise in producing his newly patented concept. The end product helped launch an industry.

The first production site was in the Platt Plow Works plant in Carthage, but the company had moved into its own two-story facility by 1895. Using the open coil springs as a resilient base for the then-popular cotton, feather, or horsehair mattresses offered the best night's sleep available. The first bedsprings, sold to retail merchants from horse-drawn wagons, were the forerunners of today's spring-filled bedding sets.

The company slowly prospered and grew. A factory was opened in Louisville, Kentucky, and the partnership became a Missouri corporation in 1901. Leggett became the first president, serving until 1921, when he was succeeded by Platt. The latter served until 1929, when J.P. Leggett, Jr., became president.

Under the leadership of F.B. Williams (1932-1935), George S. Beimdiek, Sr. (1935-1953), and H.M. Cornell, Sr. (1953-1960), the firm continued its growth. Cornell became chairman of the board in 1960, a post he held until his death in 1982. Succeeding him as president was his son, Harry M. Cornell, Jr., grandson of co-founder Leggett.

Today the younger Cornell is chairman and chief executive officer. Under his leadership, Leggett & Platt has achieved its greatest growth and success. It was he who determined that the company would become "The Components People," a manufacturer's manufacturer, supplying a wide variety of top-quality components to finished-product companies.

The strategy proved highly successful. From three plants and $7 million in sales in 1960, Leggett & Platt now has more than 80 facilities nationwide and annual sales approaching one billion dollars. A

*TOP: The names of J.P. Leggett and C.B. Platt live on in the company they founded more than a century ago. Their legacy of entrepreneurial partnership also endures.*

*BELOW: The original factory in Carthage, the Platt Plow Works, where Leggett & Platt began manufacturing bedsprings in 1883.*

Even a beatnik would give up his pad for a mattress with a Leggett & Platt innerspring construction! In fact, you'll discover that Leggett & Platt constructions are easier to sell to everybody and their trouble-free performance keeps your customers happy for a lifetime

*Leggett & Platt*
INCORPORATED

*Fortune* 500 company with approximately 10,000 employees, it has been listed on the New York Stock Exchange since 1979.

Leggett & Platt made its West Coast debut in 1968, when it acquired Signal Manufacturing Company, a Los Angeles-based major manufacturer of sleeper-sofa mechanisms. Its West Coast entry into consumer products came in 1979, when it bought Metalcraft, an Azusa manufacturer of dinette sets and bed frames.

In November 1983 the firm acquired Bedline Manufacturing Co., based in Whittier, which, as the largest supplier of hardware constructions to the furniture and bedding industry in the western United States, had been Leggett & Platt's largest competitor in those areas. Bedline remains an active and popular trade name.

In 1973 Bedline had consolidated its extensive operations into a 13-acre property that included 226,000 square feet of building space. Today that facility, at 12352 Whittier Boulevard in Whittier, is the headquarters for Leggett & Platt's West Coast Steel Division, which handles consumer and furniture products.

The company's Western Division, responsible for bedding products, is based in Cerritos. Other California facilities include a box-spring assembly facilty in Los Angeles, a spring manufacturer in South Gate, a manufacturer and distributor of bedding products in Union City, and a spring manufacturer and distributor of bedding products in Vacaville. The company also opened new facilities in Pico Rivera in 1987.

Leggett & Platt, which has about 3,500 active accounts in seven western states, is active in the Association of Western Furniture Suppliers and is a member of the Western Furnishings Manufacturers Association. Its total California employment numbers about 1,000.

From a historical perspective, the Flex-O-Lator purchase is perhaps the company's most significant one. While the Leggett family has played a major role in Leggett & Platt throughout its history, the Platts had gone their separate ways many years ago, at one point founding Flex-O-Lator, which is also based in Carthage, Missouri. The acquisition of that company thus reunited the descendants of J.P. Leggett and C.B. Platt.

Today Leggett & Platt has the same philosophy that has guided it for more than a century. Harry Cornell, Jr., describes it as " . . . this entrepreneurial feeling that has been passed down through generations of people running the company." That's how a business founded in a tiny Ozark community has become one of America's industrial giants.

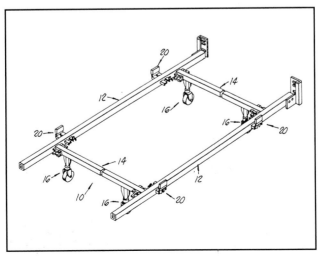

*TOP: L&P's "hip" ad in a 1960 **Bedding** magazine proves that times were indeed "a-changin'."*

*LEFT: A patent drawing of the company's Superframe, the first all-tubular metal bed-frame that features no tool assembly and adjustable box spring retainers.*

# ARCADIA CHAIR COMPANY

Casey Journigan, president of Arcadia Chair Company, describes the organization as a manufacturing business run by salespeople. "That's helped make us very customer oriented," he says. "We do exactly what we say we're going to do, and that's been a major factor in our success."

The name of the firm, which is located in Gardena, California, was bestowed on it by Casey's father, Wayne Journigan, who has lived in Arcadia for many years. Wayne and his wife, Eleanor, continue to commute to the Gardena headquarters, where he serves as chairman of the board.

Wayne Journigan purchased the company—which had been founded in 1978—in 1979, after many years of experience as a manufacturer's representative. Following his discharge from the U.S. Army Air Corps, where he served as a pilot during World War II, he began representing various product lines, including furniture. He soon formed his own company and, at one point, had a large number of contract orders for the country of Saudi Arabia.

His son, Casey, joined him in 1974, after graduating from the University of Southern California. When Wayne bought Arcadia in 1979, he ran the factory, and Casey was in charge of sales. From its original 7,000-square-foot building and four employees, the firm has expanded to 85,000 square feet of manufacturing space at several locations in the Gardena area. It has been in its present headquarters facility since 1980 and employs about 100 people.

From the start the Journigans decided that the company's niche was in executive and lounge seating. It

*Arcadia Chair Company has designs to meet every office need.*

*A side chair and an executive chair from Arcadia's Ovation Series.*

*These lounge chairs are part of the Marquis Series, which also features a love seat and sofa.*

now manufactures 20 different series, with four or five chairs in each series. The firm has also broadened its product lines to include conference tables, occasional tables, and credenzas.

True to the Journigan family tradition, the company uses manufacturers' representatives exclusively, and its products, designed primarily by nationally known designers, are sold by office-furniture dealers nationwide. The company is a member of the Business and Institutional Furniture Manu-

facturers Association.

Arcadia Chair, which is officially a division of Casey/Wayne Journigan & Associates, remains very much a family affair. Wayne and his wife, Eleanor, who kept the books for a number of years, have turned over the bulk of the responsibility to their son, Casey, and son-in-law, Chris Burgess, who serves as vice-president. Casey, who is the majority stockholder, handles sales and marketing, while his brother-in-law, who is a CPA and owns the balance of the stock, is responsible for production and finance. Burgess joined the company in 1981.

Casey Journigan is proud of Arcadia Chair Company, which has grown every year since its inception, and is proud to be a part of the furniture industry in California, where his family first settled in the mid-nineteenth century.

# HICKORY SPRINGS

Although Hickory Springs is relatively new to California, the company has a long record of growth and an excellent reputation for quality, dating back to its founding in Hickory, North Carolina, in 1944. The company, founded by Parks C. Underdown, Sr., began as a partnership, became a corporation in 1947, and is still owned by the Underdown family.

The senior Underdown served as president and then chairman of the board until his death in 1980. His son, Parks C. Underdown, Jr., is now the company president.

As a supplier, Hickory Springs' major product lines include practically everything that goes inside furniture and beds, including urethane foam, springs, bed frames, and sleeper-sofa and recliner mechanisms.

Hickory Springs is also a leader in new product design and development. In 1984 it introduced Code Red, a combustion-inhibitive foam that has become the industry standard. New recliner hardware, called zero proximity, was developed in 1987, allowing recliners to operate even when placed against a wall.

From the start, expansion has been a Hickory Springs hallmark, either through acquisition of other companies or by opening new facilities in North Carolina and in other states. The 1950s brought the Hickory Springs name to Georgia and Arkansas, followed by Tennessee, Kentucky, Mississippi, South Carolina, and Virginia during the 1960s.

Several other facilities were opened during the 1970s, primarily in the South, and Alabama was added to the list of states where the company operates. In 1981 the firm acquired Spiller Springs Company, with operations in Sheboygan, Wisconsin, and Chicago. In 1982 it built new corporate headquarters in Hickory, North Carolina, launching the revitalization of that community's downtown area.

It was in 1985 that the company made its California debut, with the formation of Hickory Springs of California, Inc., located in Bell. The following year the firm acquired United Foam. Its four plants included two in California, located in Commerce and Hayward. Among Hickory Springs' four 1987 acquisitions was Los Angeles-based American Fiber Co.

The original California facility, a metal-manufacturing plant in Bell, is now in larger quarters in Commerce, one of the company's two plants in that community. The firm also opened plants in Sacramento in 1986 and in Fresno in 1988. Today there are several hundred Hickory Springs employees in its various California locations.

After more than 40 years as primarily an eastern company, Hickory Springs came to California because of its growing importance as a furniture center. Transferred here to lead the firm's West Coast operations was Bobby Bush, Jr., who developed a management team from among local personnel. "Many of our largest customers had moved out here," he says, "and they wanted the same West Coast quality they'd had back east. That was our mission and our goal in 1985, and it remains the same today."

*Parks C. Underdown, Sr., founder.*

# MIKHAIL DARAFEEV, INC.

Mikhail Darafeev, Inc., is a family-run business dedicated to quality, craftsmanship, and innovation as seen in its Gameroom Gallery program.

Founder Mikhail Darafeev, whom the company was named after, was what used to be described as a "gentleman of the old school." He epitomized the old-world traditions and values of integrity, quality, craftsmanship, and hard work. Born in Russia, he made his way to the Los Angeles area as a young man in

*TOP RIGHT: Mikhail Darafeev, company founder.*

*BELOW: The Gameroom Gallery includes reproduction jukeboxes, fully restored antique soda machines and slot machines, carousel horses, neon clocks, and classic car sofas and bars. Photographed at Barstools, Etc., Rancho Cucamonga, California.*

the early 1950s. Unable to speak English, the young immigrant found work sweeping floors at a Los Angeles furniture factory. Eventually he worked his way up to production supervisor. The experience he gained whetted his appetite and he began to build furniture in his garage.

Darafeev borrowed $500 to start a chair frame company and moved next door to the factory that was the primary customer for his high-quality frames. In 1959 he launched Mikhail Darafeev Company, located on Whittier Boulevard in Montebello, California. His entire staff consisted of himself, his nephew, Walter Zakharov, and a couple of relatives.

Mikhail and his wife, Antonina, married in 1953, had four children: three sons and a daughter. While

Antonina stayed home to raise the children, Mikhail worked hard to build his business, learning English as he went along. His emphasis on integrity, quality, and craftsmanship paid off.

In 1969 Darafeev purchased a piece of property in Baldwin Park and erected the building that still

houses the company's main corporate offices and manufacturing operation.

Then tragedy struck. Darafeev was taken ill with stomach cancer and died in 1973. Outsiders were hired to run the firm but in a few months had put it on the verge of bankruptcy. That was when Antonina and her sons, George and Paul, took over the management of the company themselves. The next few years were difficult ones, but through perseverance and changes in marketing the firm was once again very successful.

During the late 1970s the company got away from supplying chair frames for other manufacturers and began developing its own proprietary products. Initially this consisted of occasional tables, wall units, and game sets for the residential market. Walter Zakharov, who had remained with the firm, and Paul Darafeev designed the majority of the new items. Solid oak barstools, bars, and entertainment centers were soon added to the Darafeev collection.

By the mid-1980s the company made a bold move: It discontinued the occasional tables, wall units, and entertainment centers and decided to devote 100 percent of its productive capacity to quality residential barstools and game room furniture. In this way the firm distanced itself from the lower-priced, imported furniture available for mass consumption.

The corporate gamble started to pay off the following year when sales doubled and the market for high-end game room furniture expanded. At that time repeat business and dealer referrals increased, and the company sought national distribution for the line. Since then a complete game room concept has evolved that is achieving widespread retail and consumer acceptance.

The emphasis today is on a broad range of premium-quality game room furniture, including barstools, bars, billiard tables, two-in-one poker/dining tables, and three-in-one bumper pool/poker/dining tables. Darafeev barstools are among the industry leaders, and the company holds design patents on many of its stools and game chairs.

In addition, the Gameroom Gallery by Mikhail Darafeev, Inc., also includes reproduction jukeboxes, fully restored antique soda machines and slot machines, carousel horses, neon clocks, and classic car sofas and bars.

Today rock stars, U.S. presidents, movie stars, and upscale as well as value-conscious consumers buy the products sold by Mikhail Darafeev, Inc.'s, dealers, nationally and internationally.

Antonina Darafeev and all three of her sons are active in the company. Antonina is president and chairperson of the board. The oldest son, George, is in charge of production control and purchasing; Paul, the general manager, is responsible for administration, sales, marketing, and research and development; and Michael Darafeev, the youngest son, manages one of the Gameroom Gallery test stores recently opened by the company.

These retail stores were formed to do consumer research and to test market Mikhail Darafeev, Inc.'s, products and programs. The principals believed the best way to relate to their dealers was to become a re-

tailer. Only then could they really know what consumers want, what kinds of promotions work, and how changing business conditions affect the retail demand for their products.

Mikhail Darafeev, Inc., maintains permanent showrooms in the International Home Furnishings Center in High Point, North Carolina; the San Francisco Mart; and the Dallas World Trade Center. It also sells its products to the Far East and plans to market them in Europe.

The company advertises in all the major furniture and billiard trade publications. It has also targeted high-income "connoisseurs" through specialized consumer publications. Sales leads are processed through a new, state-of-the-art automated voice mail/message center, which refers them to the dealer network.

Although Mikhail Darafeev, Inc., has made many changes and innovations from its original beginnings, the traditions started more than 30 years ago are still being carried on today. Excellence in quality and craftsmanship are of primary importance.

*Mikhail Darafeev, Inc.'s, two-in-one poker/dining table readily converts any dining area into a game room.*

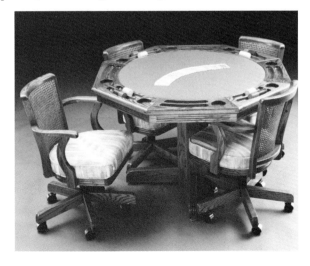

# ELLIOTT'S DESIGNS INC.

It was an unusual and seemingly unrelated series of circumstances that led Elliott and Julie Jones to launch a business from which, in the span of only a few years, a brand-new industry would spring. That industry is the design and manufacture of antique replicas of Victorian brass and iron beds. While several other companies are now in this field, the replicas produced by Elliott's Designs Inc. remain the industry standard, often imitated but lacking the quality built into every Elliott bed.

The story begins back in New Jersey, where Julie and Elliott met and married. Family ties led them to Seattle, where they stayed for a time before heading for Southern California. They went into the motorcycle business with some friends, but the love they shared for antiques led them to open an antique store in 1975, located on Pacific Coast Highway in Lomita.

Born entrepreneurs, Julie and Elliott quickly took note of the demand from their customers for antique beds. Unable to satisfy that demand with originals, they decided to begin making replicas. They opened a small foundry near their antique shop and produced their first beds in 1978, on a schedule of about 10 per week. Original antique beds were brought in from New England and castings were made, allowing the company to produce faithful reproductions. To this

day, every bed made by Elliott's is an exact replica of an original.

The beautiful beds produced by the firm were quickly in demand, forcing it to seek additional space. Elliott's moved to a 3,500-square-foot facility in Harbor City and, two years later, built a 5,000-square-foot addition. In 1981 the company moved to a 17,500-square-foot plant in Gardena, before coming to its present Rancho Dominguez location in the fall of 1983.

Elliott's moved into an existing 75,000-square-foot plant, to which have been added another 25,000 square feet of warehouse space. In a little more than a decade, it has grown from 1,000 to 100,000 square feet, from one employee to 125, and from 10 to 750 units per week. It was incorporated in 1980, with 100 percent of the stock retained by Elliott and Julie Jones. Elliott is in charge of research, development, and design, while Julie oversees the administrative, legal, and sales operations.

That original single employee, Juan Hernandez, is still with the company, and both foundry foreman Ron Thompson and factory foreman Bob Perea have served with the firm for more than 10 years. A family atmosphere is very evident, and on-

site nursery care is provided for the children of employees.

The company's products, which now include daybed reproductions in addition to its replica iron and brass beds, are sold directly to both individual retail stores and furniture chains across the United States and Canada. Elliott's has sales representatives nationwide, in addition to its showrooms in Los Angeles, San Francisco, Dallas, and High Point, North Carolina.

Elliott's products are widely recognized as the "Cadillacs" of the industry, because of the labor-intensive, painstaking care given to each item. With all operations—from foundry to steel and brass processing, from machining and painting

*TOP: Elliott and Julie Jones, who saw a demand for replicas of Victorian brass and iron beds and, in true entrepreneurial spirit, moved to fill it. Elliott's Designs Inc. remains the standard in the industry.*

*RIGHT: From one employee in 1978 to 125 today, Elliott's Designs Inc. has moved up to this 100,000-square-foot facility in Rancho Dominguez.*

to packaging and shipping—under one roof, total control is assured, and quality is the watchword. Every employee has the absolute authority to pull a unit off the line at any time if he finds even the slightest defect, and his decision is

tors. That's quite a tribute to a relative newcomer to the furniture industry.

For Elliott and Julie Jones, it was a long trek from New Jersey to Southern California, by way of Seattle. And it took awhile to go

from motorcyles to antiques to their current business. But, in true entrepreneurial fashion, as soon as they identified a need, they moved to fill it, little dreaming they were launching an industry in which they were destined to become the leader.

*The firm's emphasis on quality has made Elliott's Designs the number-one manufacturer of brass and iron bed replicas.*

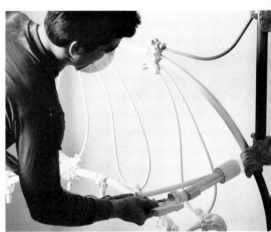

never questioned. This emphasis on quality has made Elliott's Designs the number-one manufacturer of brass and iron replicas.

The company's reputation today is such that calls come in regularly from all across the country from customers and friends who have located rusty antique beds in abandoned barns or old farmhouses. Elliott's often buys them sight unseen. When they arrive, they join the hundreds of others in that section of the plant known as The Boneyard until castings can be made from which will come yet another addition to the firm's unique line of products.

Elliott's Designs Inc. is a member of the Western Furnishings Manufacturers Association, and Julie Jones was recently named to the organization's board of direc-

# E-Z SALES & MANUFACTURING, INC.

There is an often-recurring pattern in the history of new business ventures—dreams that begin to take shape in the kitchen or dining room, the basement or garage, of the budding entrepreneur. For Julian Zambianco, founder and president of Gardena-based E-Z Sales & Manufacturing, Inc., it was none of the above. Instead, his unlikely and unusual launching pad was the crowded deck of an Ecuadoran riverboat.

It began in the late 1960s. Zambianco was an intelligence agent in South America for the U.S. government. His work required a lot of travel and he opted for the riverboats, rather than the rickety, unreliable small airplanes that were the only alternative. The boats lacked sleeping accommodations, so passengers curled up on every available bit of deck space.

The combination of heavy rains and overcrowded conditions made for long and sleepless nights, and Julian Zambianco determined to find a better way. Acquiring some rope and fishnet, he strung a make-shift hammock above the wet, crowded deck.

On arrival in Guayaquil, Ecuador, he had a supplier of fishnets make him a portable hammock, and soon his friends began asking for them. Then the entrepreneurial lights came on, and Zambianco took a few of his hammocks to local shops, where the skeptical owners accepted them on consignment. They quickly sold out, and reorders for the handmade hammocks began to pour in.

One customer, a Venezuelan tourist, persuaded Zambianco to launch an operation

in his country, where machinery to make the netting was available. As the business grew, Zambianco began to export some of his products. When the U.S. government transferred him to Mexico as a businessman/agent, he started production there. Soon, Boy Scout groups from all over Latin America became his customers. In 1969 he was contacted by the Boy Scouts of America, but the "Buy American" mood of those times prevailed, and the organization went elsewhere.

To Zambianco, that was the signal that the time had come to return to his native California. In 1970 he sold his business, resigned from his government post, and opened a small hammock manufacturing

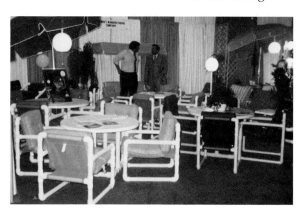

plant in Harbor City. He brought with him one hammock maker from Mexico, who, with four other men, represented the entire work force. In 1974 the firm moved to 134th Street in Gardena, then to its present 28,000-square-foot facility at 1420 West 166th Street in 1978. Today there are 30 employees and more than 60 outside contractors.

The American operation was successful from the start. In addition to the Boy Scouts of America, the customer base included such major chains as Sears, Roebuck and Co., JCPenney, and Thrifty Drug, plus sporting goods stores, Army-Navy stores, and small independent outlets. Zambianco developed a mini-hammock that weighs less than a half-pound and sells for under $10, yet can support a quarter-ton of weight. For obvious reasons, it became immensely popular.

Today E-Z manufactures and sells 34 different styles of hammocks, ranging from lightweight portable models to luxurious double-wide units. The company, which also makes beanbag chairs, patio furniture and covers, and other camping accessories, recently broadened its base with the acquisition of Oasis Canteens, which has been in the canteen manufacturing business since 1915, and Norlund Camping Axes.

The crowded deck of an Ecuadoran riverboat may seem a strange place for opportunity to come knocking, but when it did, Julian Zambianco was ready.

*TOP: Julian Zambianco (in the background), founder and president of E-Z Sales & Manufacturing, Inc., relaxing with several friends in Minihammocks on the porch of a house on Lake Tana, Ethiopia.*

*LEFT: The E-Z Sales & Manufacturing, Inc., booth at the National Furniture Market, with the outdoor resin furniture line on display.*

# TERRY HINGE AND HARDWARE CO.

Barry Silverman, founder, president, and sole stockholder of Van Nuys-based Terry Hinge and Hardware Co., is as much at home on the ski slopes, or behind the wheel of an Italian-made sports car, or at the helm of a sailboat, as he is at his desk at Terry Hinge.

Silverman has been on the go all his life. As a teenager, he made his way to the South Pacific, where he worked aboard Japanese, American, and Australian boats. Returning to Southern California, where he was born, he went to work for a wholesale hardware company that specialized in heavy oil-field equipment. Looking to diversify, the company challenged Silverman to develop some furniture industry business.

Equal to the task, he located tooling, designed some hinges, and led the firm into the shutter hardware business. The company quickly became disenchanted with this small business, and Silverman's boss suggested he take it over in his spare time.

Silverman quickly founded Terry Hinge in the garage of his San Fernando Valley home. He and his wife and a neighbor assembled the products that Silverman then loaded into his car for delivery. Within a short time, he had left the oil field equipment business and his 400-square-foot garage behind, first renting one facility and then a larger one, both in Van Nuys, before moving into the present quarters, which the company owns and which it expanded a few years ago from 30,000 to 60,000 square feet.

The product line now includes hinges for furniture, shutters, computers, pianos, and other items. The company also manufactures functional hardware, including magnetic catches, touch latches, stereo hardware, and the hardware used for ready-to-assemble furniture. Terry Hinge has about 100 employees and maintains a sales office in New York.

In 1979 Barry Silverman decided to get away for awhile from the daily pressure of running a business. So for six months he worked as a maitre d'hotel and bartender at his favorite ski resort. He skied every day and kept in touch with his business by telephone until he returned.

Silverman's South Pacific experiences had instilled in him a love for the sea and for sailing, so he purchased a home in Malibu right on the beach, bought a Hobie Cat, and went sailing every day. Today his primary hobby is racing automobiles, not the high-speed machines of Indianapolis and other tracks, but exotic vintage cars. His favorite is the Italian-made Siata, a very rare vehicle built in the early 1950s. Silverman owns three rare 208S roadsters, which he has carefully restored and which represent about 10 percent of that model in existence.

Once rare in the United States, the sport of vintage auto racing has become extremely popular, and Silverman has raced his cars all over the country and in Europe and, in 1985, won a championship in his class.

Silverman gives much of the credit for his firm's ongoing success to Don Goldman, vice-president. "Don's the one who runs Terry Hinge and Hardware Co. So when I'm off skiing or sailing or racing, I know the company is in good hands."

# VIRCO MFG. CORPORATION

It is probably safe to say that during the past 40 years a majority of people in the United States have sat on chairs made by Virco Mfg. Corporation in schools, meeting rooms, restaurants, hotels, convention centers, or government facilities.

It is not the firm's only product line, but Virco does produce enormous quantities of chairs in numerous designs. Every day, for example, it manufactures 10,000 folding chairs, 5,000 upholstered stacking chairs, and 6,000 plastic stacking chairs.

Virco is not only the largest manufacturer of classroom furniture in the United States but it also has a

*(From left) Donald Heyl, sales manager; Julian Virtue, founder; and Alan Ferl, later president and currently vice chairman, participated in ground-breaking ceremonies for Virco Mfg. Corporation in February 1950.*

market share of approximately 50 percent. It is a fully integrated operation, with the company fabricating all the parts and doing the welding, assembling, and shipping.

Virco is also among the top three firms nationwide in the manufacture of upholstered stacking chairs, as well as folding chairs and tables. Approximately 2,500 folding tables are produced daily. It also manufac-

tures computer-support furniture, juvenile furniture, and wood and steel office furniture. Annual sales are in the $200-million range.

Like so many American success stories, this one began in humble circumstances. The year was 1926. Julian Virtue and his brother, Philip, had dropped out of high school and began experimenting with chrome plating in the backyard of their home in Los Angeles. As it grew, the firm, originally called U.S. Plating Co., moved from there to a plant near downtown Los Angeles and later to facilities on West Century Boulevard.

*Julian Virtue (front row, third from right) and Philip Virtue (front row, far left) in 1923 while employees of S and M Lamp Company. Three years later, on August 26, 1926, they formed their own company.*

The company continued to grow, even during the Depression. It specialized at first in custom nickel plating for other manufacturers but then began making beauty parlor furniture, upholstered tubular steel chrome-plated chairs, and then dinette sets. During World War II it supplied bunks to the military.

In 1950 Julian Virtue left the firm and launched Virco. He began by buying Slauson Aircraft Co., which during the war had made cartridge casings. When Julian Virtue acquired it, the Slauson Aircraft Co. was making school furniture, and its only customer was the Los Angeles School Board. Under its new owner the firm began diversifying, a move at least partially dictated by the seasonal nature of school furniture sales. It introduced folding chairs and tables, and also focused on aggressively expanding its markets.

Within a few years Virco was distributing its products nationwide, and in 1954 it acquired Dunn Furniture in Conway, Arkansas. This additional manufacturing site enabled Virco to greatly reduce its freight costs and to better serve its markets on the East Coast and in the South.

Virco took a major step in 1971 when it opened a plant in San Luis, Mexico, across the border from Yuma, Arizona. Labor costs had risen sharply in the highly competitive furniture industry, and the move not only helped the firm's labor costs but provided badly needed jobs for Mexican workers. The "twin plant" or maquiladora concept is jointly sponsored by the U.S. and Mexican governments and permits American companies to operate manufacturing facilities in Mexico and import fabricated parts or finished products duty free.

Virco is now one of the largest maquiladora employers, with about 1,200 workers who perform most of the labor-intensive tasks, enabling the company to retain its competitive pricing edge. It has become Virco's second-largest facility behind the Conway plant, which has about 1,300 employees. The Los Angeles operation has some 600 workers.

When old-line furniture manufacturer Haywood-Wakefield went out of business, Virco bought part of it, taking over a large plant in Newport, Tennessee, in 1984. That facility produces melamine plastic chair seats and backs, which are then shipped to Los Angeles or Arkansas for final assembly. It employs about 200 workers.

Virco went public in 1964, its stock trading in the over-the-counter market until 1977, when it was listed on the American Stock Exchange. The Virtue family retains a major interest, however, and continues to manage the company. Julian Virtue is chairman emeritus and is active on a daily basis. He also serves on the board of directors of the Pepperdine University School of Business. Serving as president and chief executive of Virco is his son, Robert A. Virtue.

Bob Virtue began working for the company during his summer vacations while in high school and college. After graduating from the University of Southern California in 1954, he served for two years in the U.S. Navy and then joined the organization on a full-time basis.

Virco Mfg. Corporation has come a long way from the backyard of that Los Angeles house where it got its start. Today, in addition to its Mexican facility, it has factories and distribution centers across the United States and maintains sales offices in every major American city. Recently *Forbes* magazine recognized Virco as one of the best small companies in America. To Julian Virtue, $200 million in sales and a work force of 4,000 employees can hardly seem small, especially when he thinks about that backyard where it all began.

# BROWN JORDAN COMPANY

The Brown Jordan Company was founded in 1945 by Robert Brown and Hubert Jordan in Pasadena, California. As has been the case with so many other successful American companies, this one was launched in a garage. The new venture produced custom wrought-iron breakfast sets. Its first customer was Bullock's department stores. Other sales were principally to interior designers.

From the beginning Brown Jordan focused on beauty of design

*RIGHT: Quantum, extruded-aluminum furniture designed in 1982 by Richard Frinier. The Quantum lounge chair received an IDSA Certificate of Achievement in 1984.*

*BELOW: Wrought iron is prominently featured in Brown Jordan's line of furniture. This Florentine set was designed in 1987 by Richard Frinier.*

and quality of construction and its reputation, along with its sales, which grew rapidly. Brown, an engineer, was in charge of design and production, while his partner, Jordan, was responsible for sales.

The company's success with breakfast sets led to the development of outdoor dining sets, and in 1948 it introduced a line called Leisure. Designed by Brown and made of welded tubular aluminum frames and vinyl lace seating, both available in a wide range of colors, Leisure established a new category of furniture and ultimately spawned a new furniture industry.

The Brown Jordan Company long ago left that Pasadena garage far behind. Today it is headquartered at 9860 Gidley Street in El Monte, where it also has manufacturing facilities. The firm also has a factory in Newport, Arkansas. These facilities produce Brown Jordan's extensive lines of extruded-aluminum, cast-aluminum, teak, and wrought-iron furniture. Sales are primarily to high-end dealers and interior designers and decorators, for use in both residential markets and in hotels and other commercial operations.

In extruded aluminum furniture, the company's oldest and most popular line is Tamiami. Dating back to the 1960s, it was named after the Tamiami Trail, which runs across Florida, linking the cities of Tampa and Miami. Its diagonal lacing pattern gives it a distinctive appearance. Other lines of Brown Jordan tubular furniture feature pads and cushions, many of them adaptable for both outdoor and indoor use.

Brown Jordan also manufactures an extensive line of cast-aluminum furniture, available in about a dozen unique designs. Often mistaken for wrought iron, it is in fact quite different, with its own look and feel. For furniture making, aluminum has two important characteristics: exceptional strength and the ability to be cast into the most beautiful and intricate forms. This combination allows the designer to give free rein to his imagination. An example is Brown Jordan's Calcutta design, an adaptation of Thomas Chippendale's Chinese design, but in a considerably lighter scale.

Brown Jordan's cast-aluminum

furniture, with both indoor and outdoor applications, is in some of the finest homes and commercial establishments in the world. None of the company's aluminum furniture is carried in inventory but is all made to order.

The firm now markets a variety of teakwood furniture for living rooms, sun rooms, dining rooms, and for outdoor areas. Made of plantation-grown teakwood, the furniture is extremely durable, and will last for years left outdoors. The distinctive Mission style lends itself to the simple, warm appearance of the teak material. The teak collection includes a dining set, chaise lounge, sofa, love seat, lounge chair, ottoman, end table, and cocktail table.

In addition, Brown Jordan has reintroduced wrought iron to its product line. The Renaissance Collection of wrought iron has set new benchmarks for this handcrafted Italian Renaissance-style furniture. The collection includes dining groups, a chaise lounge, a sofa-settee, bar stools, a lounge chair, and accessory tables.

Brown Jordan ceased to manufacture wicker and rattan products in October 1989 due to strategic

direction changes.

The company has not only blazed a trail in furniture design but in technology as well. For example, its outdoor aluminum furniture will maintain its look for many years, even under the most adverse weather conditions, as a result of the exclusive UltraFuse finish developed by the firm. The process uses powdered paint that is electrostatically charged, guaranteeing a lasting finish. Introducing the new technology literally raised the roof at Brown Jordan; the massive equipment had to be lowered into the plant, requiring that a section of the roof be removed.

In recent years the ownership of Brown Jordan has changed hands

several times. In 1983 the company was acquired by Integrated Resources and, five years later, became a division of Chicago Pacific Corporation. In January 1989 Maytag Corporation purchased all the assets of Chicago Pacific, later spinning off its furniture companies. On July 7, 1989, Brown Jordan was purchased by Ladd Furniture, Inc., located in High Point, North Carolina.

Much has changed since Robert Brown and Hubert Jordan began their partnership in 1945, but not everything. Today Brown Jordan makes leisure furniture as it did at the beginning—by creating attractive designs and producing furniture to the highest standards of quality. Designs, styles, materials, and production methods have changed but the Brown Jordan Company remains the design and quality leader in the leisure home furnishings industry, with no intention of relinquishing that enviable position.

# WAMBOLD FURNITURE

Wambold Furniture is a company that has enjoyed fast-paced growth during its 16-year history as a maker of quality furniture, from dining room tables to entertainment centers to headboards. Greg Wambold, president, sole owner, and co-founder of Wambold Furniture, was still in high school when he enlisted in the U.S. Navy, remaining on reserve status until graduation. After a four-year tour of duty, he was honorably discharged in January 1974. One month later, with no experience in the furniture business, he and a friend from high school started a furniture company.

On February 14, 1974, the firm opened for business in a 1,400-square-foot industrial building in Chatsworth. Wambold, a second-generation Californian born in the San Fernando Valley, had some experience in metalwork from working on a part-time basis during high school. During his naval service, he had spent some off-duty hours in a woodworking hobby shop on the base and had built a few pieces of furniture.

With Wambold's limited background and a partner who had studied woodworking in high school, the two launched the company. The first product line consisted of ready-to-assemble occasional tables. The partners alternated responsibilities, with one man in the shop making furniture and the other on the road selling it.

Their marketing technique was unique. At the beginning of each week, they would load all the necessary parts and equipment into the back of a small truck, and whoever was doing the selling would begin driving the California freeways, from one end of the state to the other. When nearing a city or town, he would leave the freeway, find a telephone book, and take down the

*Greg Wambold (left) and Phil Marker, his original partner.*

names and addresses of furniture retailers. The next step was to visit these stores to show the owners photographs of the products.

When a sale resulted, Wambold or his partner rented a motel room nearby, spent much of the night assembling the furniture, and then delivered it the following morning. This unorthodox method worked extremely well, so well that before long neither partner had time to sell. They hired a salesman and began shipping the furniture to buyers.

The company's success dictated a need for more space, so the managers leased the adjoining 1,400-square-foot facility before moving across the street to a 3,000-square-foot plant. The firm had spotted a gap in the furniture business between the low and high ends and had successfully filled it. In 1975, 18 months after the business was started, Wambold's partner decided to leave the area, and Wambold purchased his interest.

The corporation's rapid growth continued. Wambold Furniture moved to a 12,000-square-foot facility about one mile away and before

long had leased several adjoining plants, for a total of 60,000 square feet. In 1985 Wambold purchased 7.52 acres of land in Simi Valley on which a 116,000-square-foot building was erected. That building is now the company's headquarters and primary manufacturing facility. But to reach the plant, Wambold had to build a new road, at a cost well in excess of one million dollars.

Even that much space soon proved inadequate, so an additional 110,000-square-foot building was leased in Moorpark. The building is used primarily for warehousing and shipping, plus all of the company's upholstery work is done there.

Today the firm produces a broad range of household case goods, mostly in oak, for the living room, dining room, and bedroom. To the original product line of occasional tables have been added audio and video units, entertainment centers, headboards, nightstands, dressers, armoires, bunk beds, hutches, china cabinets, buffets, and dining room tables and chairs, the latter being the only upholstered items the company makes.

Wambold products, which are in the medium price range, are sold primarily to major independent retailers throughout the United States

*Then and now: Wambold Furniture has come a long way since 1974, when its first product line (left) was introduced. The company's current products include dining room furniture (above) as well as living room and bedroom furnishings.*

and in Canada and Europe. The company maintains a showroom in San Francisco. A large showroom in the World Trade Center in Dallas was closed in April 1989, when a High Point, North Carolina, showroom was opened. Greg Wambold is a member of both the Western Furnishings Manufacturers Association and the American Furniture Manufacturers Association.

The meteoric rise of the firm has required enormous amounts of time and energy, plus large doses of on-the-job training. From 1,400 feet and two people, it grew in 16 years to nearly a quarter-million feet and 500 people.

The company operates two shifts, as it has since the beginning, but now Greg Wambold has lots of help. As the business grew he hired a sales manager, a controller, and other supervisory personnel. Today there is a general manager/vice-president of manufacturing who handles the operating responsibilities, submitting daily reports to Wambold, who says his philosophy is to "hire the right people and then let them do their jobs."

The firm has traditionally done all design work internally. In the early days it was mostly a matter of keeping abreast of what was hot in the market, doing some brainstorming with the sales force and then coming up with some new products. Today the system is a bit more formal. In 1986 a man was hired to do design and engineering. There is

*TOP: Greg Wambold (far left) posed with his first employees in 1975.*

*BELOW: Wambold employees in 1977.*

now a staff of eight using the latest technological advances in computer-aided design and manufacturing (CAD/CAM). Technology is also very much in evidence in the plant. A self-described "machinery nut," Greg Wambold takes periodic trips to Europe to seek out and purchase the most highly sophisticated computer-operated machinery available.

Being on the leading edge of technology and with the right people on his team, Greg Wambold now has a little more time to pursue some recreational activities. A dedicated outdoorsman, he goes moose hunting in Alaska and polar bear hunting via dogsled on the Baffin Islands at the North Pole. Other favorite fishing and hunting haunts are in Wyoming and Montana. For a time he raced professional-class drag boats, but he sold his boats a few years ago.

Challenges in life attract Wambold, whether he's hunting a polar bear or building a business. Among the things that challenge him and the rest of the staff at Wambold Furniture is growth. With the way the company has grown, that is one challenge they continue to meet most successfully.

# INNOVATIVE COMPONENTS CORPORATION

Michael Guccione, founder, president, and chief executive officer of Innovative Components Corporation, has been in the furniture industry most of his life, starting as a delivery boy at age 15. A Southern California native, he graduated from Woodbury University in 1973 with a degree in interior design. He then worked in furniture sales for several years before stepping out on his own.

Innovative Components was started in 1979 in a spare bedroom of Mike Guccione's home. His only coworker was a minority partner who handled sales. In 1986 the company, which by then had been incorporated, moved to its present headquarters at 5620 Lindbergh Lane in Bell, California. Guccione is the sole stockholder of Innovative Components, which now employs more than 40 people.

The firm supplies raw material component parts to the furniture-manufacturing industry. Those parts include drawer slides and pulls, locks, sleeper mechanisms, webbing, moldings, glass, lighting fixtures, and numerous other items. In its method of operation, Innovative is similar to a contract sales force, not fabricating any products but representing the component manufacturers and selling to manufacturers of finished goods.

Two of the 1,600 customers in the latter category are the Opus II Collection and the Avant Collection, both subsidiaries of Innovative Components. Opus II furniture is sold mainly through interior designers and decorators, while Avant furniture, which is primarily made of marble, is sold through high-quality retail furniture stores.

The company's marble comes from Italy, where it maintains a buying office in Carrera. There are two showrooms, called Innerspace, which are also owned by Guccione. One is at the Pacific Design Center in Los Angeles and the other is in San Francisco.

The Avant and Opus II furniture is designed locally and manufactured in the United States, Italy, and the Philippines. Products are displayed at Innerspace, as well as in other outlets.

Innovative Components is involved in both community and industry organizations. The company is an active supporter of the Bell Chamber of Commerce and is a member of the Western Furnishings Manufacturers Association and the Association of Western Furniture Suppliers.

Mike Guccione has come a long way since beginning his career as a delivery boy. In many ways his story is a textbook case of the successful entrepreneur—a risk taker, hard worker, and visionary who launches a tiny business in a spare room at home and builds it into a multilevel organization and a dynamic factor in its industry.

*Innovative Components' headquarters in Bell, California.*

# STØR

James D. Stadtlander had an idea. During his retailing career, the former senior vice-president/marketing for Ole's Home Centers and W.R. Grace Home Centers West had become convinced there was an untapped market for home furnishings specialty stores offering contemporary European styling adapted for the California life-style.

Stadtlander developed a business plan and took it to a former business associate named Harvey Knell, with whom he had worked at Ole's. That company, owned by the Knell family, had earlier been sold to Grace. After leaving Grace, Knell had formed a venture capital firm called Trico Capital Management. He liked the idea and agreed to finance a feasibility study, as well as help in the management process.

Stadtlander, who had been working from his apartment, opened small offices in Pasadena and hired a handful of people to assist him. When the feasibility study demonstrated that the concept was sound, fund-raising efforts began in earnest and, within six months, Knell had obtained commitments for some $13 million from several venture-capital firms.

STØR was incorporated on Au-

An artist's rendering of STØR's City of Industry store, opened on October 28, 1987.

gust 6, 1986. City of Industry was chosen as the site for its first store, which would contain 150,000 square feet of space on two levels. A lease was signed subject to financing, which was obtained in April 1987. Construction got under way immediately, and the first STØR opened for business on October 28, 1987. A second outlet, located in Tustin, was opened a year later, followed by a third, which opened in the Del Amo Fashion Center in Torrance in June 1989.

Stadtlander is president and chief operating officer of the rapidly growing company, and Knell is chairman of the board. The two men plan to open as many as 30 stores in the western United States and have several locations under consideration.

STØR provides high-quality, stylish furniture and accessories, displaying them in an environment where customers can shop for decorating ideas at their leisure. There are no commissioned salespeople and customers are free to browse and to make their own selections. There are, however, information desks in the stores for customers

LEFT: *Harvey G. Knell, chairman of the board.*

RIGHT: *James D. Stadtlander, president.*

needing assistance. Adding to customer convenience in each STØR is a supervised play area for small children and a restaurant.

Basic to this trend-setting approach to furniture retailing is a huge showroom with more than 70 room vignettes and coordinated displays, from living rooms to dining rooms, bedrooms to kitchens. Each vignette includes window treatments, floor coverings, and accessories, all available in store.

Much of the furniture is assembled at home, and customers can either take their merchandise with them or have it delivered the next day for a nominal charge. Volume buying, innovative design, special manufacturing techniques, and home assembly allow STØR to offer extremely low prices.

Jim Stadtlander sums up the concept this way: "In one location, customers can choose from the European and contemporary styles that are so popular and be assured of terrific prices. We think of this as a different approach to shopping, combining the merchandise people want with an experience that comes closer to being entertainment than the typical furniture-buying chore."

Customer response to date has demonstrated that STØR was indeed an idea whose time had come.

# DON ALDERSON ASSOCIATES

Don Alderson, founder and owner of the company that bears his name, describes himself as a "furniture artist." It seems an apt term for a man who creates, designs, and manufactures a wide range of furniture and many other functional accessories.

Alderson grew up in Chicago and attended area schools, majoring in fine arts and business. After graduation he taught college for two years and then decided to venture out on his own in the furniture business. The year was 1979. He came to California because he felt it had much to offer, both in styles and materials.

At first he worked alone, designing furniture in a studio in his home. Growth came rapidly and, before long, he found himself supervising an operation that became Don Alderson Associates, which now includes six stores and a manufacturing facility. The stores are located in Los Angeles, San Francisco, Seattle, Denver, Chicago, and Fort Lauderdale. Other stores are in the planning stages: in San Diego, Hawaii, and New York. Alderson

is also considering expanding on an international scale sometime in the future.

In addition to its own outlets, the company's products are featured in showrooms across the United States. Sales are to architects, designers, decorators, and major department stores. The many different lines of furniture include products made from hard woods, soft woods, iron, and stone. They are used in high-end residential applications, restaurants, hotels, offices, banks, and other commercial establishments.

The company features as many as 5,000 different designs, all planned to create feelings of relaxation and warmth. Don Alderson calls it "high-style casual" furniture, and the company's rapid growth is clear evidence of its popularity. The Los Angeles store, located close to Beverly Hills, numbers many celebrities among its customers.

That store, at 639 North La Peer Drive, is also the company's headquarters. Don Alderson himself

*This bedroom set from Don Alderson Associates features a Noori armoire, four-poster queen bed, night table, and chaise lounge; bamboo-and-glass console and side table; and two rattan stools.*

spends relatively little time there, although he remains involved on a daily basis in the operation of the manufacturing operation and the stores. When he is not traveling around the country visiting his stores, he can usually be found working at his home, which overlooks the Pacific Ocean at Laguna Beach. Not surprisingly, it is completely furnished and equipped with his own creations, from furniture to towel racks and from candlesticks to chandeliers.

This man from Chicago has come a long way in a short time. Today the schoolteacher turned furniture artist and manufacturer runs an organization with about 175 employees, proof positive that "high-style casual" was the right idea.

*The Coyote Bar & Grill in Chicago ordered a variety of lodgepole/pine club chairs, end tables, and dining chairs from Don Alderson Associates to convey the restaurant's southwestern theme.*

# KOSUGA FURNITURE, INC.

When Kosuga & Co., Ltd., opened a sales office in San Francisco in 1962, it was a particularly significant event for two reasons. Not only was it the organization's first facility in the United States but it took place as the firm was celebrating its 100th anniversary.

A century earlier, in 1862, Ichirobei Kosuga, the great-grandfather of the current president, began manufacturing rattan furniture and other goods in Osaka, Japan. In 1890 his son, Kyotaro Kosuga, took over the business and relocated it to Tokyo, under the name Osakaya. In 1930 the organization was incorporated and established its headquarters in Nihonbashi. Kyotaro Kosuga ran the company for nearly a half-century. In 1938 Ichiro Kosuga, son of Kyotaro and grandson of founder Ichirobei, became president.

The company continued the growth and expansion that had characterized it from the beginning, establishing factories in other Japanese cities. In 1946 it started manufacturing wooden furniture, much of it purchased by U.S. military bases in Japan. In 1956 it began exporting furniture to the United States for the first time. As it grew, it underwent several name changes, becoming Kosuga Industry Co., Ltd., in 1943 and Kosuga & Co., Ltd., its present name, in 1963.

At first the firm's activities in the United States were on a small scale. The San Francisco office had a single sales representative. Then, in 1964, it established Kosuga Furniture, Inc., an assembly plant also located in San Francisco. In 1968 the company signed a licensing agreement with two American companies, Brown-Saltman and Baby-Line, U.S.A., to manufacture their products in Japan. That was

*The Pacific Ocean provides a stunning backdrop for these Kosuga chairs.*

followed, in 1971, by a licensing agreement with La-Z-Boy, U.S.A., to manufacture its products in Japan for distribution in Asian countries.

In 1976 Kosuga Furniture, Inc., was relocated to its current facilities in Southern California, which it purchased and built at 19700 Magellan Drive in Torrance. The company did, however, retain a showroom in San Francisco, which it continues to operate.

In 1977 Yasumasa Kosuga became the fourth generation to head the parent company when he suc-

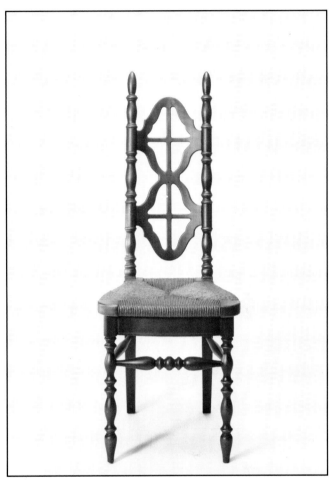

*Kosuga manufactures contemporary furniture in 10 different finishes.*

ceeded his father, Ichiro, as president. The latter continues to serve the firm as chairman of the board.

Under Yasumasa Kosuga's leadership, the company continued to expand its operations in the United States. Kosuga Hawaii, Inc., was established in Honolulu in 1978, and a year later a showroom was opened in Dallas, Texas. In 1989 the company opened a showroom in Laguna Niguel, California.

Kosuga Furniture, Inc., is under the direction of another fourth-generation member of the Kosuga family. He is Yasumasa's brother, Mitsuo Kosuga, who has been with the American company since 1970 and is now its president. Two other brothers are executives with the parent company in Japan.

Kosuga Furniture, Inc., has about 45 employees in its Los Angeles facility, where it finishes and upholsters rattan products imported from the Philippines, Indonesia, and Taiwan. It also produces dining-room and game-room chairs and tables in oak and pine, as well as living-room furniture. The firm also functions as a purchasing agent, acquiring products of other companies for use in hotels and restaurants in Hawaii and the continental United States. It also purchases furniture materials for export to Japan and finished goods from other manufacturers for its own customers. In 1988 the company became the sole agent in Japan for Baker Furniture, purchasing Baker's products and shipping them to the parent corpo-

ration for distribution.

The company in Los Angeles is a custom house, producing furniture in 10 different finishes and 200 different fabrics. Its products are distributed by more than 100 outlets, mostly high- and medium-end stores and rattan specialty stores.

The parent corporation, Kosuga & Co., Ltd., is now more than 125 years old. Under four generations of Kosuga family leadership, it has developed an enviable record of growth and success, a record that may well be unmatched by any family-controlled business in the world.

# HARPERS

*Harpers' conference room at the Pacific Design Center showroom. Displayed are Harpers' manager's chairs upholstered in black leather, as well as Series D tables with custom (black) wood tops.*

The company name is small and simple: Harpers. It was founded by Harpers, is owned by Harpers, and, for more than a half-century, has been run by Harpers. It is even located on Harpers Way in Torrance, California. But, except for the name, there's nothing small about this company.

It started out simply enough, in Philadelphia, Pennsylvania, in 1947. William Henry Harper and his 18-year-old son, Harry, started the business as an assembly operation for another Philadelphia furniture company. The senior Harper, known as W.H., had a background as a tool and die maker, a trade requiring precision and high quality, attributes he instilled in his son as the young man learned at his father's side.

For seven years the Harpers ran

*The complete line of Harpers' Series E ergonomic seating is displayed here. Also shown is a Multiple Options manager's station complemented by segmented glass panels.*

their furniture operation by day and built dies during the evening hours, primarily focusing on a die for a filing cabinet. In 1954 they sold the furniture business for $10,000, packed their belongings in a rented trailer, and headed for California.

Settling in Santa Monica, they rented a 5,000-square-foot facility and began making filing cabinets. They had no established methods of sales or distribution, so W.H. Harper made the rounds himself. These first cabinets were called "Devon." Today 18 models of storage cabinets carry the Devon name.

The firm grew, and in 1958 it moved to a 10,000-square-foot plant in El Segundo. Harry Harper did all the tool and product design and made most of the dies. Four years later Harpers introduced a line of square steel tube-leg desks. As the growth continued, two nearby buildings, each with about 5,000 square feet, were rented, doubling the company's facilities.

In 1966 Harpers began constructing its own plant in Torrance and the following year moved into the 120,000-square-foot facility, which housed its corporate headquarters, manufacturing plant, and showroom. New product lines were added, including seating, lateral files, and wood desks. Although the new quarters were six times larger than the previous ones, it only took about a dozen years for the company to outgrow them.

In 1978 Harpers purchased 25 acres of land in Torrance and began construction of a 330,000-square-foot plant, into which it moved its entire operation in 1980. Even that was to prove inadequate, and an

additional 220,000 square feet were added in 1986. Much of the recent growth was due to the company's entry, in 1984, into systems furniture, representing a comprehensive selection of multiple-option panels and components, freestanding modular desks and credenzas, electrical options, filing, and storage. This design and application flexibility is certain to make this the primary office system of the future.

Harry Harper is considered the principal driving force behind the company's growth. W.H. Harper, who died in 1981, had taught his son well. For many years Harry spent most of his time on the shop floor working shoulder to shoulder with the employees he has always considered as family. That family, which numbered about 10 in 1954, has grown to more than 700 people.

Family is a word the Harpers take very seriously. It is used to describe not only relatives and employees but dealers and customers as well. Everyone is treated as a valued member of that family, which has had much to do with the firm's growth and success.

Harpers, in addition to its Torrance facilities, maintains showrooms at the Pacific Design Center in Los Angeles and in San Fran-

cisco. It also operates sales offices in Seattle, Washington, and Dallas, Texas. The company's high-quality office furniture is sold exclusively through furniture dealers. Sales are primarily in the western states, but the firm is planning to expand its distribution throughout the United States.

Today Harry Harper is chairman of the board and chief executive officer but is less active in the day-to-day operations of the business. Much of those responsibilities are now carried by Harry's son, Hank, the third generation of Harpers to run the company. Hank came on board in 1972 as secretary/treasurer. Trained in management information systems, his first job was to computerize the company, a task that took about three years.

Hank then became director of operations, establishing what has become an ongoing process of automation, using the latest computer-aided design and manufacturing technologies. In 1984 he was named president. Serving with Harry and Hank on the company's board of di-

rectors is Harry's wife, Linda.

A Harper practice that has been faithfully continued by Hank is community and professional involvement. The company supports many charitable causes and is active in various industry groups, including the Western Furnishings Manufacturers Association and the Business and Institutional Furniture Manufacturers Association. Hank Harper is an active member of the Young Presidents' Organization and, in his leisure time, enjoys scuba diving, fishing, and underwater photography.

The people of Harpers are proud of what has come to be known as The Harper Tradition. It includes the following six characteristics: quality, reliability, predictability, stability, value, and family. Those are the foundation stones on which three generations built Harpers.

# ROBLES CUSTOM FURNITURE

Robles Custom Furniture, located at 4912 West Jefferson Boulevard in Los Angeles, is a family-owned partnership founded in 1951 by Urbano "Bano" Robles and his wife, Ofelia. It is still run by the couple and their daughter, Patricia Ruiz.

Urbano Robles began his career as an upholsterer during the early 1940s after graduating from high school. He went to work for the Model Furniture Manufacturing Company and promptly fell in love with the furniture and interior design industry.

World War II was to interrupt his career, as it did for so many thousands of other young men. In 1943 Robles, who had married Ofelia a year earlier, entered the United States Army Air Corps, where he served as a radio operator on a B-24. He was honorably discharged in 1946.

Soon he enrolled in Woodbury College (the now renowned Woodbury University) to further his education in the specialized field of interior and furniture design. He graduated in 1950 with a bachelor's degree in interior design. Robles Custom Furniture is the only manufacturing firm of its kind in the area with this prestigious credential, which has been a key factor in the success and longevity of the company.

A year later Urbano and Ofelia launched their own company servicing the Los Angeles area. Their marketing began with the restoring and reupholstering of living room furniture to the retail customers. They then expanded into custom manufacturing to the design trade only, which moved the company into larger facilities on Beverly Boulevard near Fairfax. It remained there until the mid-1960s, when it moved to its present location.

Today the firm manufactures

*Urbano Robles, president.*

high-end residential and commercial seating in its 4,000-square-foot plant, where 15 specialized craftsmen are employed. The finished products are created primarily for interior architectural design firms and interior decorators with representation in prominent design showrooms in the Melrose/Robertson district.

In April 1988 a major fire caused much damage and forced the firm to suspend operations. But a month later, after a lot of around-the-clock cleanup work and remarkable loy-

alty and support from its clients and suppliers, Robles Custom Furniture was back in business.

While Urbano Robles has turned over most of the responsibilities for running Robles Custom Furniture to his daughter, Patricia, and his wife, Ofelia, he still comes into the office every day. After all, it is not easy to walk away from a love affair that has lasted nearly a half-century.

# EXECUTIVE OFFICE CONCEPTS

When Richard L. Sinclair founded Executive Office Concepts (EOC) in 1969, he was already a veteran of 15 years in the furniture industry. Prior to developing EOC he had been president of R.L. Sinclair Associates, a leading manufacturer's representative agency with showrooms and warehouses in Los Angeles and San Francisco.

With two other people Sinclair opened a 1,500-square-foot facility in Carson, California, manufacturing office accessories made of Plexiglas, metal, and wood. EOC soon began producing case goods and, in 1976, acquired Alliance Contract Furniture, another Sinclair-owned business specializing in the manufacture of office and contract seating.

EOC moved into a large new plant in Compton in 1976, where it now employs about 200 people and manufactures an extensive line of office furniture, ranging from traditional to contemporary styles, much of it designed internally. In the past 10 years EOC has expanded its production facilities three times. In 1985 a wood veneer processing and laminating facility was added. The company also manufactured television cabinets, at a separate facility, for several major television-set makers.

EOC has long been recognized for its office furniture and was among those manufacturers on the first wave of California designs that eventually had significant national impact. Its wood furniture system, introduced in 1979, has become one of the finest in the country, on standard with U.S. government agencies and major businesses.

EOC products have received many coveted design awards over the years, including the Roscoe Award given by *Better Homes & Gardens* and an equally prestigious award from the Institute of Business Design. In addition to its creative in-house design team, there are usually several industry-acclaimed independent designers working on new EOC products. The combination has helped the company develop a reputation for high quality and creative product designs at competitive prices.

Today EOC has showrooms in New York, Washington, D.C., Philadelphia, Chicago, Dallas, San

Francisco, Compton, and at the Pacific Design Center in Los Angeles. Sales are primarily to the furniture trade through approximately 1,500 dealers and design firms nationwide. The company also operates a separate division that caters to hotels.

Founder and president Dick Sinclair, whose wife, son, and daughter are also with the firm, has long been involved in activities. He is a past chairman of the National Office Products Association and was one of the leaders in a successful campaign to modify the standards set for the furniture industry by the Southern California Air Quality Management District. The company is a member of the Business and Institutional Furniture Manufacturers Association.

Executive Office Concepts has come a long way since it began in that small Carson facility back in 1969. Today it has emerged as the largest independently owned quality wood office and contract furniture manufacturer in the western United States—and is growing faster than ever.

*TOP: Executive Office Concepts purchased this Sapeli Pommele tree for its unique veneers, which have a crystallized, marbleized look. The giant primeval tree, which measured 80 feet in length and up to 12 feet in diameter and weighed approximately 100 tons, was discovered lying in a semi-petrified state in an African forest. The tree produced 320,000 square feet of veneers, enough to cover six football fields.*

*RIGHT: Richard L. Sinclair, founder and president.*

# SENCO PRODUCTS, INC.

It was during the late 1940s that three men—a machine shop operator, a staple salesman, and a schoolteacher—were to join forces in an endeavor that was to revolutionize the way upholstered furniture is made and, at the same time, eliminate the need for a skill on which the industry had long relied, that of the "tack spitter."

The three men were, respectively, Albert G. Juilfs, who operated the Springtramp Eliminator Company in Newtown, Ohio; William Tillinghast, who had turned to Juilfs for help in filling an order for an automatic stapler; and George Kennedy, who had worked with Juilfs on the design and engineering drawings for the stapling tools.

It soon became apparent to the three men that the more profitable end of the business lay in staples rather than in tools. Joining forces under the Springtramp banner, they purchased their first staple-producing machine in 1950. The following year the company was incorporated as Senco Products, Inc., Senco having been the coded version of the original name.

One of the earliest products was a pneumatic stapler used to attach fabric to the interior shells of automobiles. But it soon became apparent that there were much greater opportunities in the furniture industry, thus sealing the fate of the "tack spitters."

There was considerable resistance at first, especially from the upholsterers, or "spitters," upon whom the industry heavily relied. The upholsterer would pop tacks into his mouth like a handful of peanuts, working one at a time to the front of his mouth and, using his tongue, placing it head first onto a magnetic tack hammer. While driving that tack home, he was maneuvering the next one into position with his tongue.

Although they worked rapidly, they were difficult to train or replace and took years to develop proficiency. It quickly became apparent to owners and plant managers that air-driven staplers were far more efficient and cost effective, and, eventually, even the tack spitters themselves grudgingly accepted them.

Today Senco, headquartered in Cincinnati, Ohio, is the world's largest manufacturer of air-powered nailers, staplers, and pinners, with its tools and fasteners distributed in more than 30 countries. The fasteners themselves range in size from one-eighth-inch staples to 3.5-inch nails. The company serves a broad range of industries, including furniture, automotive, construction, boat building, and shoemaking. In addition to its industrial fasteners, it developed a line of medical products, which the firm sold to Johnson & Johnson in November 1986.

The company first came to California in 1961 when it took over a struggling distributorship on Alhambra Avenue in Los Angeles. Today it operates six sales and service centers and has more than 200 dealers in its western division, headquartered in Orange, California. The northwestern division is located in Pleasanton, California.

Today Bill Tillinghast is chairman of the board, and George Kennedy, who serves on the board, operates a distributorship in Georgia. The third member of the original team, Al Juilfs, is deceased, but his family's involvement continues with his son, George, the president of SENCORP, who became president of Senco in 1966.

Senco Products, Inc., stands today as a tribute to the vision of three men from different walks of life who pooled their talents and their energies to launch a company whose products are known and used worldwide.

*Senco workers using an early product called a "tacker" to help overcome the negative attitudes of the "tack spitters," who saw the new technology as a threat to their painstakingly learned skills.*

# Patrons

The following individuals, companies, and organizations have made a valuable commitment to the quality of this publication. Windsor Publications, the Western Furnishings Manufacturers Association, and the Association of Western Furniture Suppliers gratefully acknowledge their participation in *California Furniture: The Craft and the Artistry.*

Don Alderson Associates*
Almac Felt Co.*
Arcadia Chair Company*
Brown Jordan Company*
Mikhail Darafeev, Inc.*
Elliott's Designs Inc.*
Executive Office Concepts*
E-Z Sales & Manufacturing, Inc.*
Harpers*
Hickory Springs*
Innovative Components Corporation*
Kosuga Furniture, Inc.*
Leggett & Platt*

Lewis Industries*
McFlem Chair Manufacturing Company, Inc.*
Monterey Furniture*
Robles Custom Furniture*
Senco Products, Inc.*
STØR*
Terry Hinge and Hardware Co.*
Virco Mfg. Corporation*
Wambold Furniture*

*Partners in Progress of *California Furniture: The Craft and the Artistry.* The histories of these companies and organizations appear in Chapter 6, beginning on page 95.

# Index